ELON MUSK

A MISSION *to* SAVE *the* WORLD

ELON MUSK

A MISSION *to* SAVE *the* WORLD

Anna Crowley Redding

SQUARE
FISH

FEIWEL AND FRIENDS
New York

An imprint of Macmillan Publishing Group, LLC
120 Broadway, New York, NY 10271
fiercereads.com

Our books may be purchased in bulk for promotional, educational, or business use. Please contact your local bookseller or the Macmillan Corporate and Premium Sales Department at (800) 221-7945 ext. 5442 or by email at MacmillanSpecialMarkets@macmillan.com.

Library of Congress Control Number: 2018955556

Originally published in the United States by Feiwel and Friends
First Square Fish edition, 2021
Book designed by Raphael Geroni
Screenshots taken by Mandy Pursley
Square Fish logo designed by Filomena Tuosto

ISBN 978-1-250-79209-9 (paperback)

10 9 8 7 6 5 4 3 2

LEXILE: 950L

For QUINN and CROWLEY

TABLE OF CONTENTS

CHAPTER 1

TAKE AWAY
the
ARMOR

Actor Robert Downey Jr. was looking at the opportunity of a lifetime. He'd just landed the role of comic book superhero Tony Stark, the billionaire genius also known as Iron Man.

Stark is not your cookie-cutter superhero. He wasn't born with supernatural powers. He is flawed, gritty, intense—driven. Just ask Captain America.

In an epic movie scene, Captain America confronts Tony Stark. Taking one stalking, provoking step at a time, Captain America circles Stark, spitting out a question meant to expose Stark's inferiority.

"Big man in a suit of armor. Take that off, what are you?"

Stark doesn't miss a beat and doesn't even bother to turn his head to look at Captain America before answering.

"Genius, billionaire, playboy, philanthropist."

Those four words not only summed up the man, but also summed up the herculean task Robert Downey Jr. had before him.

Downey had to accomplish nothing less than making Tony Stark *real*. And that meant embodying those four words: genius, billionaire, playboy, philanthropist.

Sitting across from *Iron Man* director Jon Favreau, Downey discussed the role. He needed to understand Stark's character deeply, answering questions like what made Tony Stark tick, what drove his ambitions, what kind of genius could transform fantasy into reality. Because if you understand the character, then you can *become* him, and that's how you bring Tony Stark to life.

Downey was struck by an idea. He wanted to hang out with a real-life Tony Stark.

And he had someone in mind. One man whose personality and life actually epitomized the heart and soul of Tony Stark's character, with all the trappings of Stark's supersized success. If Downy could spend time with this man, study him, try to get in his head, well then, Downey could nail the role.

That man was Elon Musk.

At thirty-five years old, Elon had already amassed a fortune and was well on his way to becoming one of the most powerful people in the world. With companies like PayPal, Tesla, and SpaceX, he pushed technology to the limit until he forced innovation and breakthrough, making his mark on three of the biggest industries that exist: banking, automobiles, and space. His ambitious ideas were so far-out that people often laughed at him, until they didn't—usually because he'd accomplished the impossible.

> **TBH:** Like Tony Stark, Elon also found time to make the rounds in Hollywood's most glamorous social scene. To be super clear, Elon explained to a *Telegraph* reporter that he was merely 10 percent playboy. The other 90 percent Elon put firmly in the "engineer" category.

In 2007, Robert Downey Jr. gave Elon a call and soon found himself walking around SpaceX headquarters with Elon himself—observing, talking, and picking Elon's brain. That time allowed Downey to perfect the role.

CHECK IT OUT! In the next installment of Marvel's big screen franchise, *Iron Man 2*, Elon would even have a cameo.

Elon Musk's cameo in Iron Man 2. *(© Marvel Studios.)*

That said, there was a major divergence between Elon and the comic book character. Tony Stark's script came with a slick backstory: *Child prodigy and heir apparent of famed entrepreneur accomplishes one incredible feat after another and then takes the helm of his father's company and pushes it to the next level and beyond.*

Elon's backstory was far from slick. His childhood was dark, painful, and brutal. Elon had to endure both emotional torment at home and physical attacks at school. As a bullied schoolboy in Pretoria, South Africa, he was not an heir apparent. He was not a media darling in waiting. No, Elon was simply trying to survive.

Elon Musk on March 19, 2004. (Photo by Paul Harris/Getty Images.)

NAME: Elon Reeve Musk

NICKNAMES: Genius Boy, Muskrat

DATE OF BIRTH: June 28, 1971

PLACE: Pretoria, South Africa

FIRST COMPUTER: Commodore VIC-20, at age 10

BOOKSHELF: *The Hitchhiker's Guide to the Galaxy*, by Douglas Adams, and Isaac Asimov's Foundation series.

GAME SHELF: Dungeons & Dragons

DAYDREAMS AND NIGHTMARES

AS A LITTLE BOY IN SOUTH AFRICA, IT WAS OBVIOUS FROM the time Elon could speak and toddle around that he was different. Elon's mom, Maye Musk, recognized her son's intelligence straightaway.

"He seemed to understand things quicker than other kids,"[1] she said.

But she noticed something else, too—something about Elon's behavior that concerned her. Elon would suddenly stare off in the distance, falling into a daydream so deep, so trancelike, that no one could get his attention. It could happen mid-conversation or in the middle of a busy room. His mother was worried. Did Elon have a massive hearing loss?

Shuffling him off to doctor after doctor, Maye tried to get to the bottom of it. The doctors saw it too. He sometimes seemed lost in another world that no one could penetrate.

Elon endured test after test. Finally, his doctors scheduled him for surgery. The plan was to remove his adenoids and hope Elon would hear better.

ADENOIDS: Adenoids are part of the immune system in infants and young children. Seated at the back of the nasal passageways, close to the ears, the adenoids' job is to help the body tackle viruses and other germs as they enter the body. But sometimes, in fighting infection, they swell. Usually, once the germ is dealt with, they shrink back to normal. But if the adenoids become too big or infected, they can block the Eustachian tubes and even affect hearing.

But the surgery had no impact at all. That's when they discovered his hearing was actually fine. It was his mind. Elon was simply so deep in thought, so focused on his ideas, immersed in every detail, that he detached from the rest of the world.

It was as if a movie was playing out before his eyes, allowing Elon to visually puzzle out a problem. Like daydreaming on steroids, he could not only see ideas but run virtual tests on them too.

"It seems as though the part of the brain that's usually reserved for visual processing—the part that is used to process images coming in from my eyes—gets taken over by internal thought processes," Elon explained to biographer Ashlee Vance. "I can't do this as much now because there are so many things demanding my attention but, as a kid, it happened a lot. That large part of your brain that's used to handle incoming images gets used for internal thinking."[2]

That was not the only personality trait of Elon's that stood out from an early age. A penchant for breaking rules and breaking them boldly—with commitment, drive, and flair—landed six-year-old Elon in some pretty hot water with his mother.

It all started when Elon's mom grounded him. She made his punishment perfectly clear: Elon would not be allowed to go to his cousin's birthday party.

And Elon's reaction was also perfectly clear. Stay at home? When his younger brother and sister were going to the party? No way. Absolutely not.

Mind churning, Elon realized he needed a plan to get around the punishment.

Wait—his bike! He could ride his bike there. Elon let his mother know in no uncertain terms that he *would* most certainly be at the party. He didn't need her to drive him there. He would ride his bike—all by himself.

Elon recounted this story in an auditorium full of people at the Computer History Museum. The crowd hung on his every word as he explained that telling his mother was a critical mistake. Because as soon as he divulged his plan, his mother looked at her son and fibbed.

"She told me some story about how you needed a license for a bike and that the police would stop me,"[3] he explained.

To a six-year-old, dealing with the police seemed really bad. So a bike would not work. As Elon saw it, that left him with one option: He would have to walk.

Only, his cousin's house wasn't around the corner or in the neighborhood or even close by. In fact, the birthday party was across town—about twelve miles away.

One foot in front of the other, Elon walked. And walked. And walked.

Some *four* hours later, victory was in sight. Elon was just a couple of blocks away when he spotted his mother leaving the party with his brother and sister.

"She saw me walking down the road and freaked out,"[4] he said.

Heart racing, Elon took off and ran into his cousin's yard. He climbed a tree, perched himself high in the branches, and refused to come down.

That sense of independence and injustice was unshakeable.

Two years later, after Elon turned eight years old, his parents divorced. Elon, along with his brother, Kimbal, and sister, Tosca, lived with their mom. A model and dietician, Maye Musk woke up each morning and got to work with modeling gigs, wellness talks, meeting nutrition clients, and managing the paperwork and scheduling that comes with running your own business to make ends meet. She was not a hovering mother; she couldn't afford to be. And there was this—she wanted her children to be independent, to understand what hard work was by watching her example, and to have the freedom to find their own way.

That left Elon with a lot of time on his hands, mostly unsupervised. He did not let it go to waste. Kimbal was only a year younger, which made them natural co-conspirators.

The two boys focused on rockets. Not just reading about them, but making them and figuring out explosives.

"I am shocked," he told *Rolling Stone*, "that I have all my fingers."[5]

When he wasn't with Kimbal blowing things up or out riding their motorbikes, Elon was reading, sometimes for ten hours a day. Often, when Elon headed into town for a shopping trip with his family, he would just suddenly disappear. One minute he was there, the next minute he was nowhere to be found—until his mom or siblings checked the closest bookstore. All the way in the back, sitting on the floor, completely lost inside a book, that's where you could find Elon.

Elon's mom would even drag him along to dinner parties if she didn't have a date. "I'd bring him to meet some interesting adults, and he'd hide a book under the table to read if they weren't interesting enough,"[6] she said.

For Elon, reading wasn't simply a pastime. He was consuming vast amounts of information, devouring books whole, and remembering every detail plucked from their pages.

"I was raised by books," he explained to *Rolling Stone*. "Books, and then my parents."[7]

And comic books. Typically when you walk into a comic book store, you look around, make your selection, pay for it, and bring it home to read. But when Elon walked into the comic book store, he read them right then and there. Not just one comic book. Not two. He read them all. Every single comic book on the rack. Every single comic book in the store. Every. One. He loved them all, but some favorites were Doctor Strange, Batman, Green Lantern, Superman, and even Iron Man.

"In the comics, it always seems like they are trying to save the world,"[8] Elon said.

Devouring as many sci-fi books as he could get his hands on, Elon discovered a similar theme. His favorites were Isaac Asimov's Foundation series, Robert Heinlein's *The Moon Is a Harsh Mistress*, and J. R. R. Tolkien's *The Lord of the Rings*.

"At one point, I ran out of books to read at the school library and the neighborhood library,"[9] he said.

Ran. Out. Of. Books. So what do you do as fourth grader when you have gone through the entire collection of *two* libraries? Well, the first thing Elon did was try to convince the librarians to order more. And while he waited for those new books to come in, he needed to do something to keep his insatiable curiosity well fed . . . he read the entire Encyclopedia Britannica from beginning to end.

He relished the information, loved knowing about the greater world and everything in it. And Elon became something of a walking, talking encyclopedia himself. If his family had a question, they turned to Elon for the answer. His sister, Tosca, gave him a nickname: Genius Boy.

That said, sometimes when people around him were talking, they might get a fact or two wrong. But Elon always knew the right answer and instantly corrected them. As you can imagine, this did not win him friends. While his younger siblings were popular and had plenty of playdates, Elon did not.

But the lack of friends did not hold Elon back from reading and obtaining as much knowledge as he could on any topic that interested him. The lack of friends did not stop him from his deep distant daydreams. And the lack of friends did not prevent him from opening the covers of a great science fiction novel and losing himself completely in the story.

The truth was, the books and daydreams helped Elon feel less alone.

It had now been two years since Elon's parents divorced. Elon began thinking of his dad, who lived alone. Something about that seemed sad to Elon, even unfair.

"I felt sorry for my father," Elon explained to *Rolling Stone*'s Neil Strauss. "He seemed very sad and lonely by himself. So I thought, 'I can be company.'"[10]

As he saw it, his mom had all three kids. Elon felt it was only fair that he go and live with his father. In the end, both he and his younger brother, Kimbal, moved in with Errol Musk.

Errol was a talented and gifted engineer, an entrepreneur, and part owner of an emerald mine. His home had plenty of books to feed Elon's reading habit. And with site visits to Errol's construction projects, Elon and Kimbal took advantage of the opportunity to roll up their sleeves and learn. Studying pipes and lines, they learned plumbing. Mixing and spreading mortar, the boys learned how to lay bricks. They added wiring, window fitting, and other jobs to their growing list of skills. That hands-on experience, combined with what Elon was reading, his ability to visualize processes, and his own intelligence, meant he quickly understood complicated tasks and engineering concepts in a way that felt innate, obvious.

"What's very difficult for others is easy for me. For a while, I thought things were so obvious that everyone must know this," he said. "Like how the wiring in a house works. And a circuit breaker, and alternating current and direct current, what amps and volts were, how to mix fuel and oxidizers to create an explosive. I thought everyone knew this."[11]

There was another perk to living with his father: the travel. Errol took the kids on amazing vacations to different countries around the world. But there was one place Elon wanted to visit more than any other: America. After all, as Elon leafed through page after page of his comic books, they all seemed to take place in the United States. If the storyline was good versus evil, then the backdrop for that battle, the stage for those save-the-world confrontations, was America. Plain and simple.

And Elon wanted to see it for himself. America was a place where anything seemed possible. It stood in complete contrast to the environment of apartheid in South Africa.

APARTHEID: A system of institutional segregation and discrimination for the sole benefit of white people. Codified into law in 1948, black South Africans had almost no escape from their horrific circumstances. During Elon's childhood, international outrage at apartheid exploded. It was a dangerous time inside South Africa, with protests, uprisings, and demonstrations often ending in fatalities. The apartheid laws were repealed in 1991.

Finally, at ten years old, Elon was sitting on a plane with his dad, headed for a visit to the land of the free.

America did not disappoint. While caped superheroes were not roaming the streets, Elon did discover something amazing in his hotel—an arcade.

Elon already had a video game player, but it was quite primitive. "It didn't have cartridges," he said. "It had four games you could play."[12]

But in America at that time, many hotels and motels had their own video game arcades, and traveling from one city to another, Elon made finding the game room a priority.

Slipping quarters into the slots, pushing buttons at rapid fire, finessing his moves, Elon wasn't just playing the games, he was puzzling out bigger questions. How do these games work, anyway? How do you program them? How do you program computers? How do you create games?

Not long after Elon returned to South Africa, Elon would get his first chance to explore his questions about video games, computers, and how they worked.

On his next trip to the local mall, Elon headed straight to the electronics store. And it just so happened, they'd received shipment of a new type of electronic—a home computer.

"It was like, 'Whoa,' Elon explained. "I had to have that and then hounded my father to get the computer."[13] Gathering up all his saved allowance, Elon asked his father to make up the difference.

THROWBACK!

Commodore-VIC 20

MEMORY: 5 kilobytes

RELEASE DATE: 1980

HISTORY: The first computer to sell one million units, it was a hit on the new home computer market. Previously, computers were sold to businesses, universities, and adult professionals. This computer was targeted to families and kids for games and education.

PRICE WITHOUT ACCESSORIES: $299.95

COMPETITIVE EDGE: Sound and color

PITCH MAN: William Shatner, as in Captain Kirk!

A Commodore VIC-20. (Photo by Evan Amos.)

Soon, Elon had a Commodore VIC-20 sitting in his house. It came with a manual for BASIC programming language—with a workbook full of lessons to practice each new bit of programming.

"It was supposed to take like six months to get through all the lessons,"[14] Elon said.

But for ten-year-old Elon? It took him *three* days. He didn't sleep, but he mastered programming his new computer. "It seemed like the most super-compelling thing I had ever seen,"[15] he said. Elon set to work trying to program his own games.

He couldn't get over it. "You could type these commands, and then something happens on the screen. That's pretty amazing."[16]

Two years later, Elon created a game called Blastar. "In this game," Elon wrote in the description, "you have to destroy an alien space freighter, which is carrying deadly Hydrogen Bombs and Status Beam Machines." Elon sold the code to a technology magazine for $500. It was his first taste of taking a new technology, obsessing over it, innovating, and then using those skills to make money.

GAME ON! A software engineer at Google has since taken the code and made the game playable online for free. blastar-1984.appspot.com.

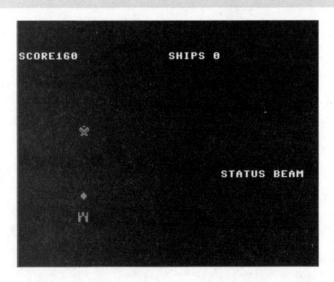

From the outside looking in, Elon had everything: a beautiful sprawling house, money, a spot in a great school, his *own computer* (at a time when that was an exorbitant luxury), and a father who shared his knowledge and time with his boys. It seemed perfect. But inside was another story—and that story was (and is to this day) dark and painful.

"It may sound good," Elon said. "It was not absent of good, but it was not a happy childhood. It was like misery."[17]

The problem, according to Elon, was his dad.

"He was such a terrible human being," Elon divulged to *Rolling Stone*. "You have no idea. My dad will have a carefully thought-out plan of evil. He will plan evil."[18]

To biographer Ashlee Vance, Elon said, "He's good at making life miserable—that's for sure. He can take any situation no matter how good it is and make it bad. He's not a happy man," he explained. "I don't know how someone becomes like he is. It would just cause too much trouble to tell you any more."[19]

Even Elon's mother would not elaborate when pressed for more detail in interviews. "Nobody gets along with him. He is not nice to anyone. I don't want to tell stories because they are horrendous,"[20] she said to Vance.

At school, Elon's situation was not any easier. He was growing up in a South Africa that celebrated macho behavior and conventional stereotypes of what it means to be a young man. But Elon was not particularly interested in sports or athletic pursuits. He was interested in technology, computers, games, and sci-fi.

Despite being at a prestigious private school, Elon found himself the target of bullies. It wasn't just that they picked on him.

"I was the youngest and smallest kid in class for years and years," he said. "The gangs at school would hunt me down—literally hunt me down!"[21]

One day at school, Elon sat next to Kimbal, at the top of a flight of concrete stairs, as a group of bullies sneaked up from behind. The gang had Elon in their sights. With every quiet, stalking step, the bullies inched closer to Elon. Finally, his head was in reach. A boy kicked Elon in the head so hard, the force sent him tumbling down the stairs, hitting step after step all the way to the bottom.

They didn't stop there. Clambering down the stairs, the boys jumped Elon and beat him until he passed out. He woke up in the hospital.

With nowhere to turn, Elon retreated into books. He opened a copy of Douglas Adams's *Hitchhiker's Guide to the Galaxy*. But Elon wasn't reading for entertainment. He was searching for an answer to an enormous question: What is the meaning of life?

BOOKSHELF! *The Hitchhiker's Guide to the Galaxy* is the first book in a comedy science fiction series by Douglas Adams. Originally broadcast as a BBC radio show in 1978, the story centers on what happens after Earth's destruction (or rather demolition), mocking modern society as it follows the adventures of a reluctant space traveler. A cultural phenomenon, the story has been adapted into a television series, a video game, a film, comic books, and plays.

"It highlighted an important point, which is that a lot of times the question is harder than the answer. And if you can properly phrase the question, then the answer is the easiest part. So, to the degree that we can better understand the universe, then we can better know what questions to ask. Then whatever the question is that most approximates: What's the meaning of life? That's the question we can ultimately get closer to understanding. And so I thought to the degree that we can explain the scope and scale of consciousness and knowledge, then that would be a good thing,"[22] Elon said later.

It was an eye-opening revelation that refueled his drive to learn as much as possible.

Elon's free time was consumed with reading, flipping through the pages of comic books, playing Dungeons & Dragons, and sitting at his computer.

GAME ON! Dungeons & Dragons is a tabletop fantasy role-playing game. Assuming a character's identity, players go on epic imaginary adventures that require problem-solving, treasure hunting, and battles to acquire knowledge. By the time Elon was in middle school, the game's popularity had exploded, with millions of players around the globe.

Dungeons & Dragons manual and game pieces. (Photo by Mandy Pursley.)

Pondering the meaning of life helped. But so did this. Elon hit a growth spurt. He shot up to six feet tall. The bullies were no longer a problem after Elon punched the toughest of them all, square in the face.

"It taught me a lesson," Elon said. "If you're fighting a bully, you cannot appease a bully. You punch the bully in the nose."[23]

If selling code for a video game was dipping his toe into the entrepreneurial waters, at sixteen years old, Elon and his brother, Kimbal, were about to wade in waist deep.

They decided to open a video arcade. Elon found a spot near his high school that would be perfect. "We had a lease, we had suppliers,"[24] he explained.

But what he didn't have was a permit. The police caught wind of it and quickly pointed that out . . . which led to something else they didn't have . . . their father's permission.

"Our parents had no idea. They flipped out when they found out, especially my father,"[25] Elon said.

Decades later, Elon and Kimbal sat together on a conference stage, still bemoaning what had happened to their arcade.

"When our parents found out, they put a stop to it—which was a real bummer because it would have been very successful,"[26] Kimbal said. Although the arcade met its end before getting off the ground, Elon and Kimbal's interest in working together survived.

But their childhood was coming to a close, and Elon decided it was time to leave South Africa to begin his life's work.

"The heroes of the books I read, *The Lord of the Rings* and the Foundation series, always felt a duty to save the world,"[27] he said.

Something big began to stir inside Elon, a mission. And that mission sprang right out of the pages of the books he was reading: Unlikely hero emerges from impossible circumstances to save humanity. And, Elon felt sure, the stage for the next part of his life would not be set in South Africa. He knew the place for his quest: America. But he did not know how he would get there.

Meet the Musks

NAME: Maye Musk (née Haldeman), Elon's mother

DATE OF BIRTH: April 19, 1948

CITY: Regina, Saskatchewan, Canada

INSTAGRAM: mayemusk

Maye moved to Pretoria, South Africa, as a toddler with her parents and three siblings. She, too, knows something about being bullied. In an interview with *1843* magazine, she recounted how she was so brilliant at math that she was often pulled out of class to show older students how to solve their math problems. This was not a recipe for popularity. But when bullies sought her out, Maye had a secret weapon—her twin sister. Kaye was athletic and stood up to the bullies. That sisterly bond remains tight.

Maye began working at the age of fifteen as a model. At college, Maye earned a degree in dietetics. Maye married Elon's father in 1970, had three children, and continued to work as both a model and dietician, while adding two master's degrees to her résumé.

In 2017 CoverGirl cosmetics named Maye an official CoverGirl. At seventy-plus years old, she has broken barriers and stereotypes about older women and how their worth, style, and sex appeal should be defined. As she put it, #JustGettingStarted.

Maye Musk at the 2018 Marie Claire Fresh Faces Party.
(Photo by Richard Shotwell/Invision/AP.)

LAUNCH

Like any superhero in the comic books he was reading, Elon needed a plan to get the one thing he really wanted: a new address in America. But his plans never seemed to work out. Arguing, explaining, negotiating, Elon tried to convince his parents to move to America—for years. And for a while, it seemed he might catch a break. Elon's dad had finally agreed to make America their new home. But in the end, Errol changed his mind. It was quite a blow.

While Errol may have changed *his* mind, Elon *never* wavered from that goal.

"Whenever I would read about cool technology, it would tend to be in the United States, or more broadly North America, including

Canada. So I wanted to be where the cutting edge technology was,"[28] he said.

And if Elon stayed in South Africa he would be forced to participate in mandatory military service for a regime he didn't believe in.

"I don't have an issue with serving in the army per se, but serving in the South African army suppressing black people just didn't seem like a really good way to spend time,"[29] Elon explained.

But how could he just move to another country and start a new life? And specifically, how could he just move to America to live, study, and work? He was South African, not American. Immigration laws didn't allow you to just show up and put down stakes.

Thinking it over, Elon's attention turned to his mother. Though she moved to South Africa at a young age, she was actually Canadian. And her father was American! Could Elon get citizenship through his grandfather? That hope was quickly dashed because his mother did not hold an American passport.

Researching immigration law, Elon kept looking for a solution. Perhaps he couldn't move directly to America, but what about Canada? Elon reasoned that if he received a Canadian passport, it would be easier to *eventually* immigrate to the United States.

Digging around in the details of citizenship law, seventeen-year-old Elon found a way out of South Africa. Because his mother was born in Canada, her children were eligible for Canadian citizenship. All he needed her to do was fill out the paperwork to get her Canadian passport, and then he could get one too. Elon filled out the forms and immediately put them in the mail. After nearly a year, Elon's passport finally arrived.

"Within three weeks of getting my Canadian passport, I was in Canada."[30]

This was no small thing. In 1989, when Elon made this trip, there was no Internet, really. You couldn't google your destination. Google Maps would not be there to help you get from point A to point B. In fact, if you wanted to travel, you usually turned to a professional travel agent. But Elon did not have that resource. His father wasn't funding this adventure; he'd only pay for schooling in South Africa. If Elon was going to make it in Canada, he had to figure it out himself: what to do, where to settle, and how to pay for it.

Sealing an envelope, Maye sent a letter to her uncle in Montreal announcing Elon's arrival. It would be great if Elon could stay with him. She waited for a reply, but by the time Elon's flight took off for Canada, she had not heard back.

Elon's plane landed and he needed to get ahold of this long-lost uncle. Plunking coins into the slot of pay phone, Elon did what everyone did back then to find a phone number: he called the operator. But the operator could not find a listing for Elon's uncle.

THROWBACK! Before cell phones, if you needed to make a call away from home or work or school, you had to use a public pay phone. They were conveniently placed in airports, hotels, some street corners, and other busy places. You held the receiver up to your ear and started putting coins into it—like a parking meter. The more money you spent the longer you could talk. Mid-conversation, the phone would alert you that your time was running out, which resulted in a sort of dance—people urgently searching pant pockets, purses, and wallets for extra coins! But there was a backup if you wanted to save your money: calling "collect." The operator would place the call and ask the person on the other end to pay for it. If you were calling your parents, this was definitely the way to go.

Elon called his mom back in South Africa.

"Collect call from Elon Musk. Will you pay for the call?"

Elon's mother took the call. And that's when she gave Elon the news. The uncle, Elon's would-be Canadian host, had moved to Minnesota. *Minnesota.*

Now what? Elon had a backpack, a suitcase full of books, and two thousand bucks. It wouldn't go far.

Elon found a youth hostel in Montreal and paid for the cheapest bed he could find.

But he needed a plan and fast. He was halfway around the world, with little money, no family, and no idea what he was going to do next.

YOU, TOO, CAN BE ELON MUSK FOR JUST $1 A DAY

WALKING AROUND MONTREAL, ELON STARTED TO COME UP with ideas. He knew that other distant relatives (whom he'd never met before) lived in Canada, but nowhere near Montreal. In fact, they lived in the province of Saskatchewan.

> Saskatchewan was home to a large community of South Africans who fled apartheid in political protest and in hopes of greater economic opportunities that were simply not possible in South Africa at that time.

Of all the options he considered, the cheapest was to buy a countrywide bus ticket and try to find his family.

Nearly two thousand miles later, Elon crossed into Saskatchewan and stepped off the bus in a tiny town called Swift Current. Once again, Elon found himself again pushing coins into a pay phone.

He dialed the number of a second cousin. No one knew Elon was coming. No one would recognize his voice. But as Elon waited for someone to answer the phone, he hoped that being family would be enough to land him a place to stay.

He was in luck. This time, his cousin answered the phone. Hitching a ride, Elon soon showed up on the front doorstep and was shown a guest bed.

Elon Musk's tweet about his time in Saskatchewan
(screenshot taken March 8, 2019).

Now, he could check shelter off the list. Next, he needed money. He'd landed on Canadian soil with around two thousand bucks. Some was spent on hostels. Some was spent on his bus ticket. Some was spent on food. It was not going to take him much farther.

So he would need to find a job to make money to feed himself and save for some kind of future, which would require an education.

Thinking it through, Elon wondered what was the least amount of money he needed to survive. Researching the cost of food, he figured he could get that cost down to a dollar a day, by purchasing hot dogs and oranges in bulk. Hot dogs and oranges. Yum.

"You can really get tired of hot dogs and oranges after a while,"[31] Elon later joked in an interview with Neil deGrasse Tyson. Occasionally he threw in some pasta, a green pepper, and even a giant jar of tomato sauce.

"So if I could live for a dollar a day," he explained, "well, it's pretty easy to earn like thirty dollars in a month."[32] Elon started knocking on doors looking for work. He tried farm work, growing vegetables and shoveling grain. He went to Vancouver, British Columbia, and wielded a chain saw as he tried logging. The most profitable post in this series of odd jobs was cleaning the boiler room of a lumber mill. But it was the stuff of nightmares.

Pulling on his hazmat suit, Elon crawled and wiggled his way through a tight underground tunnel to access the boiler.

"Then, you have to shovel and you take the sand and goop and other residue, which is still steaming hot, and you have to shovel it through the same hole you came through. There is no escape. Someone else on the other side has to shovel it into a wheelbarrow," Elon explained. "If you stay in there for more than thirty minutes, you get too hot and die."[33]

On the upside, he made eighteen bucks an hour.

Once Elon had a little bit of money, he enrolled in college.

Soon, his mother came for a visit. In addition to seeing her eldest boy, Maye was on a mission of her own—scoping out Canada and making a plan to move there.

Back in South Africa, Elon's fifteen-year-old sister, Tosca, was also getting down to business. While her mother was out of town, Tosca put the family home on the market—and sold it. Then she sold the furniture and her mother's car. When Maye returned to South Africa, Tosca asked her mother to sign on the dotted line to close the deal.

Queen's University. Kingston, Ontario. Founded in 1841. The school's motto is *Sapientia et Doctrina Stabilitas*, "Wisdom and knowledge shall be the stability of thy times."

Ontario Hall at Queen's University. (Photo by Shin.)

As Elon's classes began at Queen's University in Ontario, his mother and sister rented a small apartment less than three hours away in Toronto. As for Kimbal, he had a year of high school left and stayed in South Africa to finish. But make no mistake about it: As soon as his studies wrapped up, Kimbal intended to move to Canada as well.

Elon quickly settled into life on a college campus. Spending time talking about things like electric cars or space or any other intellectual topic he wanted to delve into, he felt comfortable. And he was meeting other students who didn't mind his know-it-all fact machine conversation style. His knowledge and drive was less out of place. It wasn't that he became the popular man about campus. But he found a place for himself and friends to share the journey. Elon bonded with his dormmate, Navaid Farooq, who also grew up abroad and had an interest in strategy games. Controllers in hand, they spent hours gaming together.

For extra cash, Elon built a little makeshift business selling computers and their parts. Tweaking this and that, he offered customized service. "I could build something to suit their needs like a tricked-out gaming machine or a simple word processor that cost less than what they could get in a store,"[34] he explained to a reporter. And if people ran into problems with any computer, he could always fix it.

Something else soon caught his attention: dating. In his second year Elon was captivated by a beautiful new student, Justine Wilson.

"She was also smart and this intellectual with sort of an edge. She had a black belt in tae kwon do and was semi-bohemian and, you know, like the hot chick on campus,"[35] he told biographer Ashlee Vance.

He had to figure out how to meet her. And Elon being Elon, he quickly came up with a plan.

Waiting outside her dorm, he "accidentally" bumped into her. He attempted small talk and even got her to agree to meet up for an ice cream.

Only, she didn't show. She was too busy studying. So he found out through friends what flavor ice cream she liked best, and then he delivered it to her as she sat behind a pile of books in the student center. And he did not stop there. He sent roses, books (since she wanted to be a writer). Justine was swept off her feet, and the two started dating.

By now, Kimbal had made his way to Canada and also enrolled in Queen's. Reunited, the Musk brothers were ready to take on the world. They figured if you want to be big in business, you better learn from the people already running big companies. And so they started by making a list of important people. Scouring the newspaper, they jotted down the names of business leaders and decision makers. And then they started cold-calling each and every one to try to set up a lunch, a dinner, a coffee, any face-to-face meeting where they could pick an expert's brain and learn something you couldn't get sitting in a lecture hall.

They called sports team owners, business reporters, CEOs, and a lot of bank executives. And one of them, Peter Nicholson, from Scotiabank, thought the Musk brothers' curiosity, drive, and pluck were absolutely fantastic.

"I was perfectly prepared to have lunch with a couple of kids that had that kind of gumption," Nicholson reminisced to a reporter.[36]

Thrilled, Elon and Kimbal took a three-hour train ride to pick Nicholson's brain. The executive was so impressed that he offered Elon a summer internship.

That summer, as Elon not only toiled away at his intern-level responsibilities, he also soaked in every detail of banking that he could. And that information didn't sit idle in his head. Elon analyzed it and summed up the entire banking industry with fresh eyes. To Elon, banks were neither nimble nor innovative. And, in his opinion, their lack of fresh, original thinking in their business was actually costing them money in missed opportunities.

"All the banks did was copy what everyone else did. If everyone else ran off a bloody cliff, they'd run right off a cliff with them. If there was a giant pile of gold sitting in the middle of the room and nobody was picking it up, they wouldn't pick it up either,"[37] he said.

Elon also learned the more pedestrian lesson of working in a real office: If an office coffee maker is labeled EXECUTIVES ONLY, an intern—no matter how self-assured or brilliant he might be and no matter how dumb the existence of an exclusive pot of coffee may seem—should not use it. Ever. Not unless that intern wants to be yelled at—the way Elon was for sipping coffee from said pot o' java.

As summer came to an end, Elon was readying for big changes. With two years of stellar coursework under his belt, Elon had applied to the University of Pennsylvania. Not only was he accepted, he received a scholarship and transferred in 1992.

The University of Pennsylvania, aka Penn, is an Ivy League school in Philadelphia. Opening its doors in 1751, the school followed the educational principles of it first president, Benjamin Franklin, one of Elon's heroes. Wharton is the university's business school.

Jon M. Huntsman Hall, the main building of the Wharton School at the University of Pennsylvania. (Photo by WestCoastivieS.)

It meant leaving his mom, brother, and sister in Canada. It also meant a long-distance relationship with his girlfriend, Justine. But it also meant he had finally made it to America.

AMERICA

NEW DIGS, NEW PROBLEMS. ELON NEEDED TO FIND A WAY TO support himself in his new country. Even with a scholarship, Elon still had expenses.

He turned to his new roommate, Adeo Ressi, and they began to scheme.

A New York City kid, Adeo Ressi returned to his hometown in 1994 and created an online guide to the city that was snapped up by America Online. Ressi continued founding successful companies and served on the board of the XPRIZE Foundation. Today he is the CEO of the Founder Institute, which trains future entrepreneurs.

Adeo Ressi speaking at the Start-up Festival 2014. (Photo by Eva Blue.)

STEP ONE: Rent a huge house. (They found a ten-bedroom house to suit their needs and got a deal on the rent.)

STEP TWO: Live in it during the week.

STEP THREE: Turn said house into a nightclub on the weekends. That's right, a nightclub.

Garbage bags darkened the windows, glow-in-the-dark paint lit up the walls, and the bass thumped hard enough to shake the ground outside. And the price to get in? Five dollars a person, which covered drinks. They had enough beer and Jell-O shots on hand to serve the more than five hundred people who showed up.

But make no mistake, this wasn't Elon wanting to party. This was business. "Somebody had to stay sober during these parties. I was paying my own way through college and could make an entire month's rent in one night,"[38] he said.

And if Maye happened to be in town visiting her son, Elon gave her a shoebox, a place to sit at the front door, and a job: Collect the money.

Elon was hitting his stride. His entrepreneurial spirit thrived, and so too did his studies.

He pursued two degrees—one in economics from the Wharton School and the other in physics, turning in papers about solar energy, digitizing books, and new breakthroughs in energy storage. These were very forward-thinking ideas that he wanted to develop and explore. In the 1990s solar energy was not at the top of the average person's mind. The world was still fixated on oil, and climate change wasn't a topic of dinner conversation in most homes. Google—who eventually started a massive book digitization project—would not even be a company for four more years.

And yet, Elon had delved into these topics with an ability not only to understand them, but to turn them into business plans.

As Elon started thinking about what he would do after college, where he wanted to make a difference, these ideas were very much on his mind.

"I thought about what were the areas that would most affect the future of humanity, in my opinion. The three areas were the Internet, sustainable energy, and space exploration."[39]

But, in theory, you can't work on all those things at the *same* time, right? So, Elon picked one: sustainable energy. And he narrowed that down to electric cars. He focused on battery storage for electric vehicles. After all, if electric cars were going to travel greater distances . . . like, say, to the next town, or have enough juice for an entire day of errands, the batteries needed to improve.

His attention turned to capacitors, which were more powerful, to be sure, but couldn't store more energy—unless there was a technological breakthrough. In that case, capacitors could get really interesting! And Elon saw the potential for just such a breakthrough.

WARNING! If you are planning to ask Elon about capacitors, be prepared. He can go on about them at the drop of a hat, with an absurd level of technical detail and something else— sheer delight. "So the area that I was studying was advanced capacitors—so essentially capacitors that have an energy density exceeding that of batteries. Because they have a very high power density but a low energy density," he said in an interview, with no notes. "So obviously if you could make a capacitor that had anywhere near the energy density of a battery with this incredibly high power density and its quasi-infinite cycle and calendar life, then you'd have an awesome solution for energy storage and mobile applications."[40] Now, try to say that three times fast! 😵

Even so, that breakthrough was a major *if* and the path to success was not guaranteed. And Elon wasn't sure success was even a possibility. As he said years later in an interview, when you embark on something, "it's desirable to figure out if success is at least one of the possibilities. Because for sure failure is one of the possibilities."[41]

He wanted to get this right. It was his future—requiring him to invest loads of precious time. Years could go by. And if you picked the wrong thing, well, you didn't get that time back.

He thought the idea and research would probably make a great topic for a dissertation, but what good would that do in the end? "So you add some leaves to the tree of knowledge," he said, laughing, "and the leaf is 'Nope, it's not possible.'"[42] That would be a bummer. And Elon's drive centered on making a meaningful contribution to humanity. It was a lot to think about. And he needed more information.

Luckily, as his final college summer arrived in 1994, he had two internships set up in Silicon Valley—a massive dose of real world experience. Working every waking hour, Elon spent his days focusing on ultracapacitors for electric cars at a company called Pinnacle Research Institute. Then, at the end of that shift, he headed to his job at the video game maker Rocket Science!

At the end of the summer, it was time to have a long conversation about what he learned, what he experienced, and what he wanted to do next. And there is no better format for that conversation than a good, old-fashioned road trip—with Kimbal. The two brothers bought a beater. To be fair, it was a BMW—but it was also twenty years old and not in awesome shape. But it would do.

"We went on a road trip from Silicon Valley to Philadelphia," Kimbal recounted. Laughing, he added, "I am younger than Elon, but we were both finishing school at the same time—because I am much smarter than him!"[43] Kimbal added that, in truth, it was Elon's *double* major that accounted for their arriving at the finish line around the same time.

Elon wasn't the only one who needed a post-college plan; so did Kimbal. Perhaps there was something they could do together. Their conversation quickly focused on an emerging technology—the Internet. In the early 1990s the Internet was new, ripe for opportunities.

Most Americans didn't even know what it was, much less what to use it for. Life was paper based.

"If you wanted to have access to a lot of information, like, you'd go to the Library of Congress," Elon explained. "Unless you were physically where the books were, you did not have access to that information."[44]

When you needed money, you drove to the bank or to an ATM and withdrew it. If you needed a phone number, you turned to a paper phone book and looked it up. If you wanted to watch a movie, you went to the theater and bought a ticket. If you needed new clothes, you drove to a store and purchased them. Life was mostly conducted in person. You did business with people and places you trusted or who had a solid reputation.

No one had any idea how dramatically the Internet would change all that.

Elon and Kimbal spent much of that cross-country drive talking about ideas, potential Internet-based businesses. The brainstorming did not stop with the road trip, nor after Kimbal headed back to Queen's, but continued the rest of the year.

And the more Elon thought about the Internet and all its possibilities, the more he did not want to miss out on the explosion of its development.

But Elon had been accepted into Stanford University's PhD program. That would mean a doctorate in materials science engineering from the mecca of technology's movers and shakers. If you were going to become a dot-com billionaire, this was the time and that was the place. The 1990s at Stanford, in the heart of Silicon Valley.

"The Internet came along, and it was like, oh, okay, the Internet. I'm pretty sure success is one of the possible outcomes. So I can either do a PhD and *watch* it happen or I can participate and help *build* it in some fashion,"[45] Elon explained.

Stanford University is located thirty-five miles south of San Francisco, in the heart of Silicon Valley. The school is known for being an incubator of tech companies. Yahoo!, Google, Cisco, Hewlett-Packard, and many more have started in the halls and dorms of Stanford. (Or nearby garage apartments!)

In 1995, Elon finished his undergrad at Penn and headed to Stanford. And on day *two* of his graduate education, Elon made up his mind. He did not want to stand on the sidelines as a witness. He wanted to be part of it.

And so right then and there, he left. On. Day. Two.

It was a gutsy move. Quit school for a start-up. And not only that, a start-up based on technology most people did not even understand. Even though Elon had some scholarships and held raves to cover living expenses in school, he still had managed to amass $110,000 in college debt.

The safe bet would have been a Stanford degree.

But Elon did not want to simply *observe* one of the most exciting technological advancements. He was willing to take a huge risk and shoot for the moon.

BOOKSHELF! *The Lord of the Rings* by J. R. R. Tolkien. Elon's vision of the future and his role in it was heavily influenced by what he read. This fantasy saga was one of Elon's favorites growing up. Like so many of the storylines that inspired Elon, this book series features an epic battle, fought by a band of heroes, who are fighting against all odds to save the world. First published in 1954–55 in three volumes, the saga became one of the best-selling novels of all time and remains popular today.

Meet the Musks

Tosca Musk. (Photo by Bloomberg/Contributor/Getty Images.)

NAME: Tosca Musk, Elon's sister

YEAR OF BIRTH: 1974

PLACE: Pretoria, South Africa

The baby of the Musk clan, Tosca also has her family's trademark entrepreneurial spirit and talent. She is a successful film director and producer and has launched a subscription movie company called Passionflix, which streams original movies and other content adapted from romance novels. Tosca has twin children at home in Los Angeles and was inspired by her mother, Maye, who worked from home when all three kids were small. Her mother taught her the value of hard work and gave her a front-row seat to running a business.

What does Tosca think of her eldest brother? "Elon has already gone to the future and come back to tell us what he's found."[46]

TYPING VS. WALKING

As Elon and Kimbal settled into Silicon Valley, ready to tackle the Internet, Elon started thinking back to his internship. There was this super awkward moment that stood out. A guy showed up at the office. He was a Yellow Pages salesman.

THROWBACK! "Let your fingers do the walking." That was the catchphrase for an advertising powerhouse called the Yellow Pages.

The Yellow Pages was a giant phone book full of listings of businesses' phone numbers and addresses. Cracking open the hefty paperback, you could thumb through to the right page and then drag your finger down the columns until you landed on the business you were hunting for—thus "let your fingers do the walking."

If your roof had a leak, there was no Internet to turn to for customer ratings of roofing companies. You opened up the Yellow Pages and picked one from the listings.

You could get a free alphabetical listing of your business. But if you wanted even more attention? You could spend bigger bucks on an ad that filled a little slice of the page or even a whole page if you could afford it. And the phone company gave all of their customers a free copy of the phone book, which made it a very popular place to advertise.

So, Elon watched the Yellow Pages sales rep fumble his way through a pitch on all the different options for listings, ads, and rates. And then a sort of verbal train wreck unfolded when the guy had to get through his spiel about a brand-new option, an *online* listing.

Sorcery! This was the 1990s. The web was in its infancy. Even national news outlets struggled to explain it to their viewers. And this salesman clearly didn't understand it either. But Elon got it.

Sure, there may not have been a lot of web pages yet. And connecting to the web was super clunky, usually over a hard-wired phone line. But as Elon and Kimbal were talking about this Yellow Pages incident, they suddenly had an idea.

What if you could offer businesses online listings that were connected directly to a map? That way, customers could find a business, see where the business was located, *and* get turn-by-turn directions. Remember, this was long before Google Maps, so it was a very forward-thinking concept.

Ready to make their mark on the Internet, Elon and Kimbal started with the Yellow Pages—by *replacing* them online.

COULDA. SHOULDA. WOULDA. Elon applied for a job at Netscape, an Internet goliath most famous for its web browser. But Netscape missed its chance to snap up Elon Musk. Elon says he never got a reply. So he thought he'd try talking to someone in person and, résumé in hand, headed straight for Netscape headquarters. But Elon only made it as far as the lobby. His nerves took over, and he turned around and walked out the door. Today Netscape is out of business.

They needed a name for their new company and came up with Global Link Information Network. It wasn't exactly catchy. And Internet companies of the 1990s needed a catchy name. After all, this was cutting-edge technology, not a two-hundred-year-old company. So as soon as they had money, they hired a marketing firm to help brainstorm a better name and settled on Zip2.

Elon would work on coding the project while Kimbal took on sales and marketing. They had the expertise to pitch the idea and the ability to explain it to people who were just beginning to understand what the Internet was and how it could help get more customers.

So in 1995, Zip2 became an official, real live start-up. Elon and Kimbal approached the business with limitless devotion, often working through the night and spending as little money as possible. Their office was a total nightmare. It was a small cube. No elevator. The toilets were not reliable. And they had one computer. One. During the day it was Zip2's dedicated web server. At night, Elon used it to program.

It was a bit of a challenge, especially since the Musk boys also *lived* in this tiny office. Luckily it was walking distance to a YMCA where they could shower every day. It also meant they didn't have to rely on their car—which could not be relied on!

ROAD TRIP ALERT! Zip2's office was at 430 Sherman Avenue, Palo Alto, California. Be sure to check out the corner of Page Mill Road and El Camino Real. This is where a wheel fell off Elon and Kimbal's beat-up BMW. As in the axle actually dug into the road.

"When we first started out, I think our ambitions were really quite low. It was really to make enough money to pay the rent,"[47] Elon said.

"For me the worst part," Kimbal said, "was eating at Jack in the Box three times a day."[48] They tried to rotate which items they ordered from the menu to achieve some variety. According to Kimbal, during a 3 a.m. Jack in the Box run, exhausted, he was downing a milkshake. That's when he spotted something funky in it. But he wasn't about to give up the milkshake or go out and get another. He reached into the cup, pulled out the unidentified ickiness and tossed it over his shoulder, and—wait for it—kept drinking the shake.

There was another entrepreneur-to-be not too far from Elon's stomping grounds: Larry Page. A PhD student at Stanford, Larry would soon begin work on the tech that would become Google. Larry and Elon became fast friends, and remain so to this day. In those early days of friendship, they would relate to working in less-than-ideal offices. Larry Page and Google cofounder Sergey Brin set up Google's first offices in the dorm and then a garage. By 2018, Larry Page was worth $54.3 billion. Google's parent company, Alphabet, was valued at $749 billion.[49]

Still, their start-up costs would quickly outpace the early money they'd managed to get from angel investors.

ANGEL INVESTOR. When you first start a company, you need money to fund it. Enter angel investors. Angel investors are wealthy individuals who give you money to get a project off the ground. Sometimes, friends and family become angel investors. Sometimes other entrepreneurs will take on the role. What do angel investors get in return for their investment? Usually, they get a small piece of the company, or equity.

"More than half of the venture capitalists we met with did not know what the Internet was and had not used it,"[50] he said. "They would literally ask, 'Isn't that something the government and universities use?'"

Elon's response? "Uh, for *now.*"

At one point, an executive picked up a hefty copy of the Yellow Pages and hurled it at Elon and Kimbal, shouting, "Do you ever really think the Internet is going to replace *this*?" Kimbal remembered looking at him and thinking, "This guy is screwed."[51]

The Musk brothers really understood and saw something few people did. And they would not give up.

Knocking on door after door to drum up business, Zip2's newly expanded sales team heard "no" after "no" after "no." No one was signing up. But they kept hitting the streets, perfecting their presentation and pitch, and eventually some car dealerships bought Zip2's service.

What was the special something that finally made the difference? It was Elon. Business owners weren't just buying into any online business directory, they were buying into Elon, into his superhuman drive to *will* the business into success.

It didn't hurt, either, that people were starting to figure out the possibilities of the Internet.

Remember that web browser company Netscape we talked about

earlier? Well, Netscape went public in August 1995 and its share price had skyrocketed by the end of the year.

"And then whether or not somebody knew what the Internet was, they knew that you could make money on the Internet somehow, even if it's on the greater fool theory,"[52] Elon explained.

THROWBACK! Netscape launched its Navigator web browser in December 1994, and it quickly became the preferred way to surf the web. When the company went public nine months later, the stock was offered at $28. Within hours, its price had shot up to $74.75 a share. By December 1995 shares were trading as a high as $171.

The Musk brothers went looking for another round of funding in early 1996. A week later, Zip2 attracted a $3 million investment from the venture capital firm Mohr, Davidow. Three million dollars.

"We thought they were crazy. Like why would they do that?" Elon said, laughing with Kimbal years later. "They obviously did not realize we were sleeping at the office!"[53]

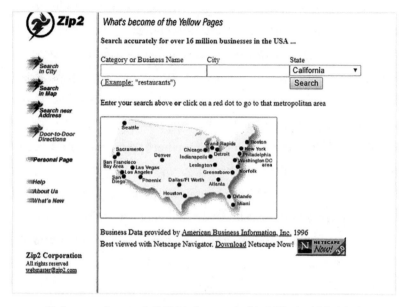

Zip2.com on January 3, 1997 (via Internet Archive's Wayback Machine).

But that money came with strings attached. Strings that would dictate who ran the company, and it wasn't going to be Elon. Instead of being CEO, Elon was named the chief technology officer.

> **ROAD TRIP ALERT!** New money meant a new, bigger office. Their new address: 390 Cambridge Avenue, Palo Alto.

Justine and Maye soon paid a visit to the new offices, and as Maye listened to employees talk about the business, she offered up a great idea of her own: Why not offer reverse directions as well! So they did. And it was a hit with users. (It was good they visited when they did. Eventually, the company would grow so fast that they crammed too many desks into the office—inadvertently blocking the women's restroom.)

As the company grew, the team came up with a game-changing plan. They would target newspaper companies.

Newspapers were at the top of the media food chain at that time. There were only a couple of twenty-four-hour news channels. Most people either subscribed to a newspaper that was delivered to their home every morning or they picked one up on the way to work. If you wanted in-depth reporting, this is where you turned. And many people read several newspapers a day.

But the papers weren't just about news. In the back, they had listings, called classified ads, where you could list your car for sale, post a job opening, offer piano lessons, etc. These ads were a key reason to buy the paper, and the money generated from them was a major source of revenue for newspapers a day.

That entire business model was about to be turned on its head.

The Internet had huge potential for telling people what was going on in the world. You didn't have to print a paper. You did not have to physically edit news video together and air it on television. The Internet offered immediacy in a way the world had never seen.

And while people were still trying to figure out how to use the Internet back then, it was clear: This new technology posed a major threat to newspapers. If you wanted to know what was happening at 2:00 p. m. around the world, why would you wait until tomorrow morning to find out?

If newspapers didn't figure out how to take advantage of the Internet, they were going to be history. The first thing newspapers needed to fix was their own websites. They needed to shift from thinking of them as little more than virtual business cards and more of a virtual newspaper, including the listings.

Elon recognized this. He and Kimbal knew their technology could help.

Zip2 sold their software directly to newspaper companies—which would allow newspapers around the country to create their own listings for their advertisers. This would make the online versions of newspapers relevant. And best of all, newspapers didn't have to reinvent the wheel. Zip2 did it for them.

It was a smashing success. Zip2 added customers like the *New York Times* and large media companies like Hearst and Knight Ridder, which owned newspapers across the country.

In 1999, Zip2 was sold to Compaq Computer for $307 million. Elon bagged a whopping $22 million from the deal, and Kimbal got a $15 million payday.

The four years leading up to that sale had been grueling. The hours, the effort, the problem-solving—all of it grueling.

"The way I like to think about it is, I was like a dog in a cage getting beaten for four years, and then they let me out, and here are all the T-bones you can eat. So it was a very weird experience," Kimbal explained, saying that he had thought he was building a company for life. "And then they give you lots and lots of money in easy-to-carry bags."[54] Kimbal was ready to make his exit from Silicon Valley.

Packing up his belongings, Kimbal headed for the East Coast. "What else do you do when you have enough financial resources to do whatever you want?" he said. "I always wanted to learn to cook, so I enrolled in a cooking school, one of the top schools in the country, in New York City."[55]

While happy the company ultimately did so well, Elon, too, had endured a grueling experience. For one, looking back on the financing deal that made him chief technology officer instead of CEO, Elon decided he would not let that happen again. He simply *had* to be in charge going forward. He was not content to simply oversee and drive the technology. He wanted to run the show.

And now he had the confidence to make such demands. After all, he and his brother had started Zip2 from nothing, and now they were multimillionaires. Not only that, the Musk brothers had shaped the way people used the Internet.

ELON'S BIG SPLURGE: A McLaren F1 sports car. Price tag? $1 million. Justine got the first ride. But—yikes! alert—not long after he bought the car, he wrecked it while showing it off to PayPal cofounder Peter Thiel.

A Silver McLaren F1. (Photo by Joe Cheng.)

And now with his bank account in pretty good shape, twenty-seven-year-old Elon needed to answer a big question: What next?

NO ISLAND PARADISE

I KNOW WHAT I'LL DO WITH MY MILLIONS. I'LL START A company with a fantastic idea: online banking. Like banking, only over the Internet.

This idea was completely out of left field. Banking was something you did in person at a physical building. It was part of your daily or weekly errands. You pulled up to the bank and walked in with your paper check in hand. Then you smiled at the people who worked there, who you saw multiple times a week. When it was your turn to talk to one of them, they called you up to the counter by name. And then they began moving your paper-based money around. That's how things worked. In person. Based on trust. Based on reputation. While ATMs were in use, allowing you easy access to your money, this technology was not yet universally accepted. And you still had to physically walk or drive to an ATM. If there was a problem, you headed *inside* the bank to get it quickly resolved by a real, live human.

This was money after all, nothing to take crazy risks with.

But something else was also happening in 1999: That new thing called the Internet was starting to really become a Thing. A year earlier Larry Page and Sergey Brin launched Google. Amazon had been selling books online for four years. And other e-commerce shops were popping up everywhere.

> **LINGO ALERT!** If you dropped the super hip term "e-commerce" into conversations, you were obviously in the know! Even though all it meant was using your computer to buy and sell stuff!

Even so, paying for things that you bought online was difficult and a little spooky—a far cry from the brick and mortar experience. First, your options were limited. You could write a check and put it in the mail. You could give someone your credit card number over the phone—which felt risky. You just hoped you were talking to someone who wasn't going to steal it.

Or the biggie: You could type your credit card number into your computer and check out online. No people involved at all. That was a leap many were not ready to take.

Even the banks themselves were not sure how to solve this problem for customers.

This was no surprise to Elon.

Remember his college internship where he learned not to use the executive coffeepot? That was where he picked up his opinion that the banking industry was not on the cutting edge of new technology or new thinking. What had been incredibly frustrating as an intern suddenly seemed like an enormous opportunity.

And now, with his bank account full of cash, he was ready to bet $12 million, more than half of his Zip2 payday, on the idea that the Internet could revolutionize banking.

> **TAKE AWAY THE ARMOR:** Should entrepreneurs invest their own money in their start-ups? That was a question put to Elon during a talk at a conference. His answer: "I think it's worth investing your own capital in what you do. I don't believe in the 'other people's money' thing. If you are not willing to put your own assets at stake, then you shouldn't ask other people to do that."[56]

In 1999, Elon decided to start a new company, a fully online self-service bank. People could open checking and savings accounts, make deposits and withdrawals, and move money around—without leaving home or the office. As long as you had a computer with an Internet connection, you could log on to your bank account.

Elon named his new company X.com. People thought he was nuts. If folks were not comfortable making even the smallest of purchases over the Internet, how on earth were they going to hand over their entire bank accounts? To the doubters, there was simply no way anyone was going to bank online. Not to mention that Elon's banking experience was as an *intern*. But Elon did not let the complexity of the banking industry scare him off. He believed in his ability to make this company a success and revolutionize the entire industry.

Elon began tackling the banking learning curve by reading as much as he could. He attracted a top-notch engineer and two finance guys as cofounders and hired an experienced team to get the company off the ground. Before the site went live, though, just five months after he started the company, personality clashes and philosophical differences caused his cofounders to walk out the door.

ROAD TRIP ALERT! X.com's first office was located at 394 University Avenue, Palo Alto.

Scrambling, Elon rebuilt the company, hired new engineers, and poured himself into the task at hand. Finally, on November 25, 1999— the night before Thanksgiving—the site went live. X.com became one of the first online banks on the planet. For Elon, heading home to eat turkey and spend time with his family was not an option. No, a meal with all the trimmings would have to wait. Elon spent the next forty-eight hours at the office. He had to make sure that everything ran smoothly and that any problems were quickly solved. Silver lining?

Elon's around-the-clock presence allowed his engineers a few hours at home with *their* families.

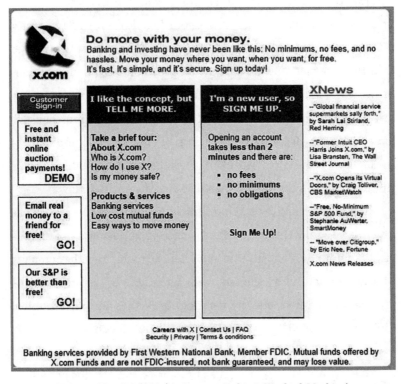

X.com on March 1, 2000 (via Internet Archive's Wayback Machine).

TBH: Sometimes hard work smells bad. According to early X.com employee Julie Ankenbrandt, the office smelled of sweat, body odor, and—wait for it—leftover pizza.

As for that gamble about whether people would actually hand over their money to an online bank? Well, as it turns out, Elon was right. People could, would, and still do bank online. The company underwent explosive growth and shaping, adding a modern twist on an ancient custom: *electronic* person-to-person payment. Before then, when someone wrote you a check, and you deposited it into the bank, it took days to process and show up in your account. This was different. This was instant.

"After the first month or so of the website being active," Elon explained to Sal Khan during a talk at Khan Academy, "we had a hundred thousand customers."[57]

> **TAKE AWAY THE ARMOR:** Starting a company? Elon says the quicker you can provide people with something they can see, the better. Whether a sketch, a mock-up, or a demonstration, find a way for people to envision your project or product.
>
> "In the beginning there will be few people who believe in you or in what you're doing," he explained. "But then over time, as you make progress, the evidence will build, and more and more people will believe in what you are doing."[58]

While Elon had been busy with his companies, Justine had focused on writing novels that would soon be snapped up by publishers. She and Elon had managed their long-distance relationship, and now she joined him in Silicon Valley. They were sharing a home, building a future together.

And in January 2000, Elon and Justine got married. While others saw Elon as brilliant, hard-charging, and relentless—Justine had additional insight into who he was.

"I don't think people understand how tough he had it growing up," she explained to journalist Tom Junod. "I was a really lonely kid and he was a really lonely kid and that's one of the things that attracted me to him. I thought he had this understanding of loneliness—how to create yourself in that."[59]

Back at work, the intensity stepped up to a whole new level. Two other Silicon Valley entrepreneurs, Peter Thiel and Max Levchin, had been working on a similar concept at a different company called Confinity. The two companies became fierce competitors. But that spring, in March 2000, they agreed to join forces, and the companies merged.

SPOTLIGHT: Jeremy Stoppelman was an X.com engineer. He would go on to become the CEO of review site Yelp.

Elon remained the largest shareholder of the now expanded X.com and also became the CEO. Even though the company soon had more than one million customers, the office culture was in deep trouble. The merger may have produced one company. But in terms of how the employees got along, it was like trying to make two rival high schools put aside their differences and become one big happy family. It didn't go well. They disagreed on just about everything—including the best software to run the business. It was so bad that Confinity cofounder Peter Thiel walked away from the company altogether.

Elon may have been running a company that had huge internal issues, but he also had a new bride whom he had yet to take on a honeymoon. Nine months had passed since they said, "I do." So in September, the newlyweds boarded a plane to Sydney, Australia.

And while the plane was in the air for the long-haul flight, a group of Elon's employees made their move. They pushed him out as CEO and brought back Peter Thiel to run the company. The honeymoon ended as soon as Justine and Elon landed and learned what happened. But Elon couldn't change it.

Peter gave the company a new name: PayPal. Elon remained an adviser to PayPal as a board member and continued to invest his money in the company.

Peter Thiel and Elon Musk at the X.com corporate headquarters on Oct. 20, 2000. (Photo by AP Photo/Paul Sakuma.)

In July 2002, eBay bought PayPal for $1.5 billion. Elon pocketed $180 million after taxes.

People were asking Elon what he was going to do next.

Remote island, palm trees? No.

String of islands and mega yacht to trot between them? No.

Spend his money on his every whim? No.

Years later he explained his choice like this. "The idea of lying on a beach as my main thing sounds like the worst. That sounds horrible to me. I would go bonkers," he said. "I'd be super-duper bored."[60] He didn't need to retreat into early retirement. Nor did he need a job. He needed to make a difference to humanity. Again.

FUN FACT: When Elon says, "Vacations will kill you,"[61] he means it. No, really. He's talking about that time he almost died of malaria. He and Justine traveled to South Africa, and Elon got the most dangerous kind of malaria. It almost killed him, but after ten days in a California intensive care unit, Elon survived.[62] His full recovery took six months.

Meet the Musks

Kimbal Musk (second from left) and his wife, Christiana Musk (third from left), at the World Economic Forum 2018. (Photo by Foundations World Economic Forum/Boris Baldinger.)

NAME: Kimbal Musk, Elon's brother

DATE OF BIRTH: September 20, 1972

PLACE: Pretoria, South Africa

After the sale of Zip2, Kimbal moved to New York to pursue his passion: food. He enrolled in the French Culinary Institute, and shortly after graduating, Kimbal witnessed the horror of the 9/11 attacks.

He lived near the World Trade Center, and quickly began cooking for the firefighters, keeping them fed as they searched the rubble for survivors and worked to extinguish the inferno. "These firefighters would come from the most traumatic places you can imagine and they would sit down and eat and come back to the real world,"[63] he said. Kimbal showed up day after day for six weeks. It was a pivotal experience because he saw firsthand the critical connection between community and food—a link he views as vital. Creating that connection in other places became his mission.

The common thread in his approach is locally grown food, prepared and shared with a strong sense of community.

Kimbal's efforts to spark a food revolution also mean bringing farm-to-table concepts directly into schools, providing schoolyard gardens to teach science and to feed the students. He has started a chain of restaurants that create connections to the community through locally sourced foods and regular support of schools, as opposed to impersonal eateries that serve food that's trucked in. His idea is that garden, restaurant, farmer, and customer are all connected.

Today, Kimbal lives in Colorado and is a father of three. He also sits on the board of Tesla and SpaceX.

Kimbal's advice for entrepreneurs centers on something a friend of his and Elon's said: Starting a business is like chewing glass and staring into the abyss. So, it's wise to choose something you really enjoy, Kimbal says. "It's a very important lesson. Do what you are passionate about because no matter what you do, if it's making a difference, it's super hard to do it. So you had better be passionate about it."[64]

CHAPTER 4

ONE PLANET IS NEVER ENOUGH

Planet Earth may be called the Goldilocks Planet—not too hot, not too cold, plenty of water, organic molecules, just right for life—but the future of the planet is no fairy tale.

Earth is at risk of a life-ending asteroid strike. And global warming, as the name suggests, could heat the planet to the point that humans' habitat is destroyed. And then there's the threat of nuclear war or some other man-made disaster. And if that's not enough to ponder, at some point in hundreds of millions of years, the sun will boil Earth's oceans.

For Elon, it doesn't matter that these events could happen in millions of years or in fifty, nor whether it's a long shot or a sure bet.

"I mean something bad is bound to happen if you give it enough time,"[65] he said. And Elon sees that as a huge problem.

A problem that has weighed on his mind for years. In 2001, as he began contemplating what to do with his time, he kept thinking about this problem in particular. The more Elon thought about it and studied it, the more convinced he became that there was only one solution: Humans needed to colonize other planets. And they should start with Mars.

Image of Mars taken by the Hubble Space Telescope on June 6, 2001.
(Photo by NASA and the Hubble Heritage Team [STScI/AURA].)

"If we were a multi-planetary species, that would reduce the possibility of some single event, man-made or natural, taking out civilization as we know it, as it did the dinosaurs," Elon said in an interview with *Rolling Stone*. "There have been five mass-extinction events in the fossil record. People have no comprehension of these things. Unless you're a cockroach or a mushroom—or a sponge—you're..."[66] Well, to paraphrase, you have no hope.

WAIT, WHAT FOSSIL RECORD? If you talk to paleontologists, this term is going to come up. It means all the information gained from fossils found in sedimentary rock. Pulled together, these discoveries tell us about the history of life.

That kind of complex problem, those kind of stakes, and the herculean effort required to save the day, well ... Elon was no stranger to that plot. He had read it over and over again in hundreds (maybe even thousands) of science fiction novels and comics as a kid. Couple that with an education in physics, experience running a company, and confidence ... Elon was ready for takeoff.

OASIS

SO NOW WHAT? THAT WAS SORT OF THE CRUX OF THE conversation that Elon had with his old college roommate/nightclub partner-in-crime, Adeo Ressi.

They had spent the weekend in New York's ritzy Long Island playground: the Hamptons. Driving back to Manhattan, they were shooting the breeze about the whole Mars thing. At first, Adeo thought Elon was kidding.

But by the end of the ride, it was clear that Elon was most certainly not joking. Elon needed more information. He dove headfirst into a pile of books. When he wasn't reading about space, Mars, or how to get there, he was calling up the world's leading aerospace experts and hounding them with questions.

He turned to NASA. Makes sense, right? The National Aeronautics Space Agency was synonymous with all things space. After all, this was the agency that put humans on the moon.

"I was trying to figure out why we'd not sent any people to Mars. Because the obvious next step after Apollo was to send people to Mars."[67]

Scouring NASA's website, he found nothing.

And that really shocked him.

But to understand why NASA wasn't running full throttle on a crewed mission to Mars, you have to revisit moments like what happened on January 28, 1986. Seven crew members waved as they boarded the space shuttle *Challenger* in Cape Canaveral, Florida. The world was particularly fascinated because one of the crew members was a schoolteacher, Christa McAuliffe.

Across the country, televisions were rolled into classrooms on carts, so students could watch the liftoff. None were as excited as Christa's own students, who gathered in the school auditorium to witness their teacher make history.

You can imagine the applause and cheering as the shuttle's engines ignited, the thrill of watching the spacecraft climb toward the heavens.

Then one minute and thirteen seconds into flight, the *Challenger* exploded. The space shuttle broke apart on *live* television. News reporters fell silent. Students watched in shock and confusion. But the violence of the explosion left little doubt. No one could have survived.

SPACE DISASTERS AND MISHAPS

JANUARY 27, 1967: Electrical fire sweeps through command module of *Apollo 1* during a preflight test. Killed: Astronauts Virgil "Gus" Grissom, Edward White, and Roger Chaffee.

JANUARY 28, 1986: Space shuttle *Challenger* explodes seventy-three seconds after launch. Killed: Astronauts Francis "Dick" Scobee, Michael Smith, Judith Resnik, Ellison Onizuka, Ronald McNair, Gregory Jarvis, and teacher Christa McAuliffe.

AUGUST 22, 1993: Mars Observer probe, costing $813 million, disappears right before it was to enter Mars orbit. Suspected cause: leaky valve.

SEPTEMBER 23, 1999: Mars Climate Orbiter, costing $125 million, is lost when it enters Mars's orbit too close to the Red Planet's surface. Cause: math mistake by engineers who failed to convert measurements from English to metric.

February 1, 2003: Space shuttle *Columbia* breaks up while reentering Earth's atmosphere. Killed: Astronauts Rick Husband, William McCool, Kalpana Chawla, Laurel Clark, David Brown, Michael Anderson, and Israel's first astronaut, Ilan Ramon.

The painful and dramatic disaster gave the public and the U.S. government a sobering example of the inherent risk of space travel.

As the grim reality sunk in, it was tough to keep people excited about space exploration, and that made it harder to keep the space agency well-funded.

Though NASA's space shuttle program resumed after a two-year hiatus, the fervor and focus on space travel waned. No longer united by the no-holds-barred desire to beat the Russians in space, the nation moved on.

But some fifteen years later, Elon was convinced Americans should be pushing the envelope, reaching for Mars. So Elon and Justine packed up and moved to Los Angeles, to the heart of America's aerospace industry.

Writing a check for five grand, Elon attended a fund-raiser for the Mars Society, where he met other space fans and sought out as much information as he could. He broke down the humans-stuck-on-Earth issue into smaller problems to solve. At the top of the list: getting the public's support. As his reading, research, and connections began to coalesce, he formed a plan.

MARS SOCIETY: This nonprofit organization is committed to exploring and colonizing Mars. It was founded in 1998 by Dr. Robert Zubrin, who has a master's degree in aeronautics and astronautics and a doctorate in nuclear engineering.

"I came up with this idea to do so-called Mars oasis, which was to send a small greenhouse with seeds in dehydrated gel that upon landing, you hydrate the gel. You have green plants on a red background," he explained. "The public responds to precedents and superlatives. So it would be the first life on Mars. The furthest that life's ever traveled, and you'd have this money shot of green plants on a red background."[68]

Despite being an engineer, an Internet guy, an entrepreneur who could rattle off obscure details about any subject he studied, Elon also had the gift of finding ways to rally the public behind his goals. And he understood the power behind an image.

A single image could change the public's mind, focus, and fill their courage reservoir. And with those horrifying and spectacular space disasters, there would be no going to Mars without tremendous courage.

Now he had to look at his bank account and figure out if he could afford it, using *his own* money. He decided that he was willing to spend half of it, even if the whole thing failed.

Elon knew it was a gamble. After all, the aerospace industry chokes down millions of dollars as a midmorning snack. It was a crumb, a token. But if the result was that the public started thinking about space exploration again, getting excited about it, he would count that as a win. And if the worst that could happen was losing money, he could stomach it.

So he got to work.

First, he needed to buy some rockets. And they weren't cheap.

"The Boeing Delta II would have cost sixty-five million dollars each," Elon said. And he wanted two. "And then I was like, whoa, okay, that breaks my budget right there."[69]

*The Boeing Delta II rocket carrying the Mars Odyssey spacecraft, April 7, 2001.
(Photo by NASA/KSC.)*

THE WAY

THOUSANDS OF MILES FROM CALIFORNIA, ELON FOUND himself sitting in a room with padded walls. It was not a mental hospital. This is where the Russians had brought him to talk rockets.

"You talk to people, who know people, and pretty soon you are talking to the Russian rocket forces,"[70] he said.

Elon had boarded a plane and flown to Russia to buy a couple of ICBMs (intercontinental ballistic missiles). Not just any ICBMs, but the largest ones in the Russian fleet. He hoped to snap them up for $10 million apiece.

"They thought I was a bit crazy. But then they read about PayPal and said, 'Okay, he's crazy, but he has money,'"[71] Elon said. He brought Adeo Ressi along as well as a space expert he'd gotten to know while studying Mars.

"This was when it was still the Wild West over there," Adeo explained to *Esquire*. "I mean, there were like dead people on the side of the road. We got pulled over multiple times, at gunpoint, and had to bribe the police. No reason. Just 'Give us money.'"[72]

The negotiations required a second and third trip to Russia. But in February 2002, that third meeting changed Elon's course. One of the Russians began shouting at Elon, spit flying out of his mouth as he yelled. "It was a strange experience,"[73] he said, laughing at the memory.

But that moment, bathed in flying spit, is when it hit him. The price of the rockets was silly, made up. That number had nothing to do with the cost of actually making them.

Why not just build a rocket, a world-class rocket, and build it for less money?

It also hit him that America's will was not the problem.

"I was actually wrong about my first premise, that there was a lack of will. In fact, I think there is a tremendous amount of will in the United States for space exploration. Because the United States is essentially a nation of explorers," he explained. "What really matters is having a *way* . . . I need to work on the way."[74]

As Elon flew back to the United States, he took all the information he had consumed about rocketry, space, propulsion, and started tapping away on his computer. He was building a spreadsheet to figure what it *actually* cost to build a rocket. First question to answer: Why are rockets so expensive?

Then, what are the materials I need to build a rocket?

What's the most cost-effective way to do it?

How should it be designed?

Where are the parts made?

If you say a rocket is made of aluminum, titanium, copper, carbon fiber, Elon explained, "you can break it down and say, what is the raw material cost of all these components? And if you have them stacked on the floor and could wave a magic wand so that the cost of rearranging the atoms was zero, then what would the cost of the rocket be?"[75]

Elon had just crossed over from buying a rocket to *building* a rocket. And that meant he needed to quickly become an expert in rocket science. Rocket. Science.

Sure, he'd blown up model rockets as a kid. And then received a grown-up physics degree. But it was not a degree in aeronautics or astronautics. Once again, Elon found himself eyeballing a massive learning curve—and jumping right in.

> **BOOKSHELF!** Elon read these and more. *Ignition! An Informal History of Liquid Rocket Propellants* by John D. Clark; *Fundamentals of Astrodynamics* by Roger R. Bate, Donald D. Mueller, and Jerry E. White.

Adeo was taken aback. "I was like, 'Whoa, dude. Let's use the Socratic method. *I got screwed by the Russians* doesn't equal *Create launch company.*'"[76]

Adeo and some of Elon's other sincerely concerned friends gathered to convince him not to do it. Too much money. Too much risk. A rocket company? You? Nope.

"A friend of mine made me watch a video of rockets blowing up,"[77] Elon said. He thanked his friends and let them know he was moving forward with his plans.

In the middle of all this professional excitement, Elon found himself completing a decade-long journey. Taking his place with thirty-five hundred other immigrants at the Pomona Fairplex, Elon rose from his seat. With Justine there to cheer him on, Elon placed his right hand over his heart and took the oath of citizenship. He no longer just lived in America. Now he was an American.

And in May 2002, Justine gave birth to a baby boy, Nevada Alexander Musk.

As the couple settled into life with a newborn, Elon continued devouring book after book about rockets, space, aeronautics. The new father continued talking to experts. Immersing himself in every piece of information he could get his hands on, he also assembled a top-caliber team to help him with the next step.

In June 2002, to the sound of a celebratory mariachi band, Elon launched Space Exploration Technologies, SpaceX for short, with the mission "to revolutionize space technology, with the ultimate goal of enabling people to live on other planets."[78]

Soon the spoils from PayPal would fund this multistep mission. First, SpaceX had to build a rocket, then use the rocket to launch paying customers' satellites into space. That revenue would fund more research and development, with the hope of getting the company closer to its ultimate goal of reaching Mars.

> **ROAD TRIP ALERT!** The address of the first SpaceX headquarters: 1310 East Grand Avenue, El Segundo, California. Its seventy-five thousand square feet wasn't much to look at, but Elon quickly gave things a sleek look with shiny concrete floors and all-white walls.

"It may seem odd that I would start SpaceX with an expectation of failure. But bear in mind that my initial thing was essentially to do essentially a philanthropic mission with zero percent chance of success from a financial standpoint," Elon explained, referring to his photo idea of green plants on a red background. "It would have effectively been a donation to the cause. So anything better than that is a win."[79]

Three months after SpaceX opened its doors, a mechanical engineer named Gwynne Shotwell stopped by to see a buddy who worked there and get a tour of the place. That tour turned into a job. Gwynne was quickly hired and became employee number eleven.

Her job was to sell SpaceX's services, like ferrying satellites to orbit, only this was years before SpaceX built its first rocket.

"Selling rockets is all about relationships and making a connection with these customers. When you don't have a rocket to sell, what's really important is selling your team, selling the business savvy of your CEO—that's not really hard to sell these days—and basically, making sure that any technical issue that they have or any concern you can address right away," Gwynne explained during a TED Talk interview with Chris Anderson.[80]

Elon's efforts were no longer about drumming up support for NASA. This was now about getting to Mars his own way and bringing the public with him, first in spirit and ultimately in the flesh. And that required successful technology and successful sales.

LOSS

IN 2002, AS THE PAYPAL SALE WAS ANNOUNCED AND ELON worked to solve the problems of making a rocket from scratch, Elon's home life took a devastating turn.

Elon and Justine faced an unspeakable tragedy. At ten weeks old, their son died of sudden infant death syndrome (SIDS). They had put Nevada down for a nap in his crib, carefully putting him on his back. And when they returned to look in on their napping boy, he wasn't breathing. Nevada was rushed to the hospital. After three agonizing days on life support, there was no hope. He could not be saved.

The medical team placed Nevada in Justine's arms so she could hold her son as he passed away. The loss was crushing.

For Elon, the only way to cope was to immerse himself in work and the complexities of engineering a rocket and building a company.

"He doesn't do well with dark places," Justine explained, while describing this part of Elon's personality to *Esquire* magazine. "He's forward moving and I think it's a survival thing with him."[81]

Elon made himself available to SpaceX 24-7, personally weighing in on engineering problems and even rolling up his sleeves and physically doing some of the work or testing when required. He now understood the technology and the problems well. His expertise, ideas, and hypotheses were essential to research and development, as well as production.

BOOKSHELF! *Red Mars* by Kim Stanley Robinson. This science fiction novel hit bookstores in 1993 and made a big impression on Elon. At its core, this book explores what is required to settle the Red Planet, in terms of science, technology, and engineering.

PAGING TONY STARK

ONE OF THE PERKS OF PUTTING YOUR ROCKET FACTORY IN A huge industrial space is the building comes with huge cargo bays. They meant Elon didn't have to stop at simply driving his (repaired) McLaren *to* work. How pedestrian! No, he could drive his car *into* the factory! Now, that's much more of a statement.

Elon's goal when he started SpaceX was to launch the first rocket in fifteen months, um . . . you know, from scratch to fully baked rocket in fifteen months.

His plan went something like this. Approach rocketry from square one, a clean slate, a blank page—well, you get the picture. Rethink everything about what a rocket is and how it comes to be and then settle on the best path forward. Which leads to starting a *rocket* company in June 2002! Then, he needed to assemble a team of top-notch engineers, computer scientists, machinists, welders, electricians, a sales team, and other employees who would work side by side to solve very hard and complex engineering problems and then launch said rocket by November 2003 to worldwide acclaim!

All in fifteen months. Whoa. Make no mistake about it, this was an aggressive goal that would demand a punishing schedule. Elon and his team were going to work nearly around the clock.

That being said, Monday through Friday, at 8:00 p.m., the team stopped work, took up positions at their computers, and blew off a little steam with the boss—trading reality for first-person shooter games against each other, *Quake III Arena* and *Counter-Strike*. Despite their best efforts to duck the rain of virtual fire, they often lost to Random9, also known as Elon Musk.

COWS IN SPACE

SETTING UP THE WEB CAM, THE SPACEX TEAM WANTED TO be sure to capture every move.

They were testing rocket engines at a three-hundred-acre test site, in a remote part of Texas that happened to be surrounded by cattle farms.

And the cows were captivating. Sure, an unbelievably loud and fiery rocket engine is cool too. But the cows.

It happened every time. Engine ignites, cows start herding. Nudging, pushing, urging their calves together into a clump—then the adult cows formed a ring around around them, standing guard. Every. Time.

A little levity helped with the incredibly tedious task at hand. Developing rocket engines requires firing them regularly so engineers could observe and measure things like vibration, temperature, power, and other performance variables. Analyzing the data, they pinpointed what needed to be retooled back in California, and the engines would be tested again in Texas.

SpaceX was working on the Merlin engine for the booster, which provides the power to lift the rocket off the launchpad, *and* the Kestrel engine, which powers the second stage of the booster.

LINGO ALERT! Fairing. In a rocket standing on the launchpad, the cargo is placed in the top, inside the nose cone. That cone is covered by the fairing, or a thin metal shell. During orbit the shell opens, separates from the spacecraft, and falls away.

Close-up of Merlin engines (© SpaceX).

As SpaceX worked on manufacturing a fairing, fuel tanks, and the rest of the rocket, that ambitious launch date sailed on past without an actual launch.

In February 2003, NASA suffered another space shuttle disaster. The space shuttle *Columbia* broke apart over Texas on reentering the Earth's atmosphere. The shuttle program was put on hold for two years, but the disaster spelled the end of the program. In 2004, the president announced that once the International Space Station was completed, the remaining space shuttles would be retired. (The last shuttle flight was July 2011.) Supplies for the space station would be delivered on unmanned cargo ships operated by European and Japanese space agencies, and astronauts would have to hitch a ride on Russian spacecraft. That is, unless SpaceX could help.

A successful rocket launch would have created a marketing and media frenzy. But SpaceX simply wasn't ready yet.

Still, Elon came up with a plan to get the government's attention. After all, the United States government was a critically important potential client. Never mind that SpaceX had launched exactly *zero* rockets. This was a sales issue, and Elon understood that. Have a demo!

So, in December 2003, Elon parked a prototype of his rocket outside the Federal Aviation Administration's headquarters in Washington, D.C., introducing the world to Falcon 1, a rocket named after Han Solo's *Millennium Falcon* in *Star Wars*.

The follow-up to his big trip was an even bigger announcement. SpaceX would begin work on a second, more powerful rocket.

Meet the Musks

NAME: Justine Musk (née Wilson)

DATE OF BIRTH: September 2, 1972

HOMETOWN: Peterborough, Ontario, Canada

JOB: Author of science fiction, fantasy, and horror for young adults and adults

WEBSITE: JustineMusk.com

Justine Musk. (Photo by PatrickMcMullan/ Contributor/Getty Images.)

PUBLISHED BOOKS: *BloodAngel* (2005), *Uninvited* (2007), and *Lord of Bones* (2008)

AWESOME GIFT: As an author, Justine adores books. One year, Elon gave her a nineteenth-century copy of *Pride and Prejudice.*

The Musks went on to have five more boys: twins Griffin and Xavier in 2004 and triplets Damian, Saxon, and Kai in 2006.

The couple divorced in 2008. While sharing custody of their five boys, Justine continues writing, giving TED talks, and blogging about her work, life, and realizations along the way.

CHAPTER 5

TWO COMPANIES

and a

FUNERAL

On a sunny California summer day in 2002, the haunting sound of a bagpipe rose from the front of a funeral procession. A white hearse and a long line of cars crawled along behind the kilt-clad player in a slow somber journey. Mourners exited their cars and piled in under a tent next to flower arrangements. The hushed crowd listened as the eulogy began.

"She died before her time," one mourner said. "And in perfect health."[82]

Only the funeral was not being held for a person. Instead, mourners were gathered to mark the death of General Motors' electric car: the EV1.

Produced in the late 1990s, the EV1 was available for lease only to a limited number of customers. These drivers weren't just signing up for a new car. They were signing on to a movement to change the way humans get around the planet—a way that didn't destroy humans' habitat.

The EV1's arrival did not escape Elon's notice. "I thought that the big car companies would develop electric cars because it's obviously the right move,"[83] Elon explained. California was even requiring that a small percentage of cars sold be pollution free by 1998. So when the largest car company in the world debuted the EV1 in 1996, Elon felt sure the EV2, 3, and 4 would come next. He couldn't have been more wrong.

When lawsuits forced California to relax its rules in 2002, car-makers quickly halted production of electric vehicles. But they did not stop there. Not even close. "GM recalled all of the EV1s and crushed them into little cubes,"[84] Elon said.

EV1 customers tried to keep their cars; they even sent checks to the company to buy them, but GM just returned their money.

"It's crazy. When is the last time that you heard about any company's customers holding a candlelit vigil for the demise of that product." He paused. "Particularly a GM product!"[85] His mind was blown.

Elon noticed something else. Devoted, loyal EV1 customers could not simply buy another all-electric car. There wasn't anything remotely similar on the market.

ROAD TRIP ALERT! A few EV1s are on display in various museums around the United States, including one at the Smithsonian National Museum of American History in Washington, D.C.

"And what makes it super insane," Elon said in an interview, "is that we are going to run out of oil anyway. It's not like there is some infinite oil supply. We are going to run out of it. So we know we have to get some sustainable means of transportation no matter what."[86]

Remember, Elon was thinking about electric cars all the way back in college. In fact, even when Elon was lingering over dinner with a date, he would go on and on about electric cars.

"It probably wasn't the best strategy,"[87] he laughingly admitted years later.

Nope. But clearly that passion for electric cars ran deep, and now Elon was having a eureka moment. "There needs to be a new car company that comes in and shows that it can be done,"[88] he said. That meant the car would need to be *long* range, high performance, and look great.

And just like with rocketry, Elon started asking around, reading, and exploring the idea in his mind.

So battery cost was an issue. But, as Elon discovered, new advances in battery technology held huge promise within reach. That being the case, he wondered, was there room for new thinking on how to make electric cars?

On the other hand, Elon was already at that very moment, um . . . taking on *rocket science.*

Both the car industry and aerospace industry were giants. Taking on groundbreaking change in both arenas, running day-to-day operations for both, seemed impossible.

"Since I was doing SpaceX, I knew that if I did try to start an electric car company *and* run it, it would be extremely painful to run two companies,"[89] he said. Never-ending work weeks, managing two different staffs, solving the worst problems of both companies.

But in 2004, there seemed to be another option. Elon heard about an electric car start-up. Their vision? Build all-electric, high-end

sports cars, using lithium-ion batteries. So far, so good. But even better? The company was named after one of Elon's childhood heroes:
Nikola Tesla.

> Born in 1856, Nikola Tesla was a famous inventor. His curiosity
> began as a child—experimenting, tinkering, and testing his
> ideas. As an adult, his innovations in electricity, wireless
> technology, and much, much more made him a household name
> and important contributor to humanity's progress. Increasingly
> reclusive and eccentric in later life, Tesla died at age eighty-six—
> alone and broke, in New York City. But more than two thousand
> people attended his funeral. His vision and contributions were
> truly ahead of their time.

Elon met with the founders, Martin Eberhard and Marc Tarpenning. Like Elon, the two men had just made millions by starting their
own company, NuvoMedia—which produced one of the world's first
handheld e-readers in 1998. They sold their start-up two years later
for $187 million.

> **ROAD TRIP ALERT!** At this point, Tesla Motors was located
> in a run-down 1960s office building, occupying an office just big
> enough for a couple of desks. You can drive past Tesla's humble
> beginnings at 845 Oak Grove Avenue, Menlo Park, California.

And just like Elon, instead of running off to buy an island, Marc
and Martin went in search of a problem to solve.

It didn't take long to settle on oil. Marc had seen firsthand oil's
influence on politics in the Middle East. And in the United States,
what was the main use for oil? Millions and millions of gas-hungry
beasts also known as automobiles.

So if that was the problem, what was the solution? Electric cars.

And not just any old electric car, a luxury sports car—which, in 2003, was absolutely unheard of.

Electric cars at this point definitely had a certain vibe, and that vibe was low budget, granola, and dorky. Think of a souped-up golf cart. You didn't drive one to feel like the coolest person on the road. (At least you scored huge points for trying to save the planet.)

Marc and Martin sat across from Elon, trying to persuade him to invest in their company. Usually these types of meetings go down like this: You present your idea, your plan, your technology. You face a torrent of questions. And then you ask for money. It's super stressful and not without awkwardness. Yuck.

But this meeting was different. Marc realized he was actually *enjoying* himself.

"The person on the other side of the table is doing something even crazier," he said about Elon. "He's building rocket ships! It was great."[90]

At the end of the day, Elon handed over $6.5 million, which made him Tesla's largest investor.

It goes without saying that Elon brought some heavyweight engineering and entrepreneurial chops to the table. But he also brought connections. And Elon was connected to a man named J. B. Straubel.

Elon had met J. B. several months earlier when J. B.'s colleague brought him along to help pitch an idea for electric aircraft to Elon. At lunch, J. B. happened to mention his own groundbreaking idea.

At this point electric cars couldn't go too far on a single charge. You could drive to work or a friend's house, but an electric car was not road trip material. J. B. had an idea for solving that problem.

Back when J. B. studied energy systems engineering at Stanford University, he converted an old Porsche into an electric car—and promptly set a world record for electric vehicle acceleration. That said, it could only travel a distance of thirty miles. Fixing that issue became J. B.'s obsession.

After college, J. B.'s day job was working on motors for a hybrid car company, and then he moved on to work for a company developing an electric-powered plane. But one night his old pals from the Stanford solar car team began gabbing about lithium-ion batteries.

"We wondered what would happen if you put ten thousand of the battery cells together. We did the math and figured out you could go almost one thousand miles,"[91] J. B. said.

This is the idea that J. B. mentioned to Elon. Elon loved it, and so after his meeting with the Tesla founders, he urged J. B. to see them. Marc and Martin hired him straightaway.

> **TBH:** When Straubel was a little boy, he took over the basement of his family home and turned it into a lab for tinkering, mixing chemicals . . . experimenting. And his face shows the evidence of his lifelong interest in pouring liquids from one beaker into another—after an explosion sent flying glass shards into his cheek, leaving a nasty scar behind.

J. B. Straubel (right) receives Deloitte's Technology Fast 500 recognition for Tesla being number one on Deloitte's list of fastest-growing technology companies in 2012. (Photo by Steve Jurvetson.)

Martin was named CEO. Marc became the chief financial officer, and J. B. was chief technology officer. As Tesla's largest stakeholder, Elon was made chairman of the board.

Ian Wright was also a cofounder. Marc and Martin brought him in, but he would only stay for a year. After leaving Tesla, he has continued to work in the electric vehicle industry.

Tesla was about to do what the big car companies refused to do . . . give drivers an all-electric car that didn't make you feel like dork driving it. Their target market: high-income people who drove luxury vehicles.

Once again, Elon knew failure was a very strong possibility. And again, just like with SpaceX, he felt the stakes were too high not to try at all.

NOT YOUR GRANDMA'S CAR COMPANY

THE AUTO INDUSTRY IS NOT KNOWN FOR WELCOMING newcomers. Ford Motors? Started selling the Model T in 1908. General Motors? Selling cars for more than a century. Honda Motor Company? Founded in 1948. And the list goes on. These companies occupy sprawling campuses, manufacturing facilities, and salesrooms across the United States. One Ford assembly plant alone covers five million square feet.

Tesla Motors, on the other hand, was the new kid on the block. Only Tesla wasn't on the block or anywhere near the block. The heart and soul of America's auto industry was Detroit, Michigan.

Everyone assumed Tesla would move there, develop key connections, and snap up top talent. They were mistaken. Tesla was, in fact, hiring, but it was recruiting from *Silicon Valley,* not Detroit.

And here's something else. The big car companies sold their cars through dealerships, but Tesla's research showed that people *hated* dealing with car dealerships. So, Tesla would take a different path and sell its cars directly to the customer.

Tesla wasn't going to be your grandmother's car company.

Elon's investment was enough to get them off the ground. But they would need other investors. And the way to get other investors? Give them an idea of where you are headed by demonstrating your idea. They needed to build a prototype.

This car would need to take people's breath away. A sleek, sexy, cutting-edge design paired with mind-blowing performance. The task ahead was clear: prove to the world that an electric vehicle could be completely, totally, and utterly awesome. They had a lot of work ahead of them.

DESERT

IN AUGUST 2004, ELON GOT BEHIND THE WHEEL OF AN RV, steered toward the open road, and headed for Nevada. Sure, he had two start-ups to worry about, but it was time for Burning Man. And he wasn't going to miss it.

Burning Man is a huge event in the Nevada desert. The pop-up community is built by the people who attend. Thirty-five thousand people came in 2004. The point? Build community, take on social issues, freely express yourself while following ten principles like self-reliance, self-expression, inclusion, and, oh, leave no trace. The desert needs to look as it did before anyone showed up! Team building and cooperation are essential to building a temporary community in extreme desert conditions. That particular year, they endured dust storms, rain, and intense heat. The event continues to grow every year and is also a favorite with Elon's pal from way back, Larry Page of Google.

Luckily, Elon had company for the hours-long trip: one of his South African cousins, Lyndon Rive.

Elon's mom had a twin sister, who had three boys and a daughter about the same age as Elon, Kimbal, and Tosca. Some of Elon's happiest childhood memories are of playing and getting into trouble with his cousins. Remember that birthday party Elon was forbidden to attend when he was a little boy? That was for one of his Rive cousins.

Now they were all grown up, and they had a lot to talk about. Like Elon, the Rive boys were entrepreneurs. It ran in the family. Lyndon had started his first company at only seventeen. Then he moved to California to join his older brother Russ, and they started a software company called Everdream, which allowed "companies to maintain their computers remotely."[92] Soon his brother Peter also joined the effort.

After developing the business, they were starting to think about an endgame, which probably meant selling the business to a bigger company and moving on.

It's that last part that weighed heavy on Lyndon's mind during that road trip: how to move on, what to do next.

Rumbling along endless miles of open road, Elon and Lyndon were brainstorming to pass the time and settle on a plan. Like Elon, Lyndon wasn't looking to start just any ol' company. He wanted to do something that made a difference.

Elon had an idea: solar energy.

"Even if you have electric cars, you have to have the other side of the equation and so how do you produce energy in a sustainable way?"[93] Elon explained. And the answer to that questions was solar.

Elon pointed out that, in his opinion, the solar industry was focused on tinkering with and improving the panel's technology, instead of solving the industry's biggest challenge: how to get solar on as many roofs as possible. How do you do that? And then what? Can you connect them, create solar grids? And manage that network?[94] That last question tied into the Rive brothers' expertise.

Lyndon was excited and started talking to his brother Peter about it.

Elon offered his cousins money and any guidance they wanted, if they would run the company. He believed in their entrepreneurial talent.

And now, with that out of the way, they could enjoy Burning Man.

BRICK BY BRICK

TESLA NEEDED A BIGGER WORK SPACE TO ACTUALLY BUILD a car and accommodate their growing team. They quickly moved into a ten-thousand-square-foot industrial building and got started— with, um . . . one toolbox, furniture from IKEA, and a few computers. But that space wouldn't be so empty for long.

> **ROAD TRIP ALERT!** Check out Tesla's first car-making space: 1050 Commercial Street, San Carlos, California.

The warehouse was quickly outfitted with a proper car lift, machine tools, and lighting. The walls and floors were painted white. Suddenly the place buzzed with activity.

> **OFFICIAL MISSION STATEMENT:** Tesla's mission is to accelerate the world's transition to sustainable energy.

Brick by brick, the team immediately set to work building a "mule," or a rolling test platform. Wait, bricks? Yes. Battery bricks. The engineers carefully stacked and glued the lithium-ion battery cells together into so-called bricks. It was the first time this had ever been done.

For the basic frame of the car, they turned to a luxury sports car. "We used a highly modified Elise chassis,"[95] Elon said.

Developed in 1995, the Lotus Elise was a two-seat luxury sports car. Not only fast, it was sleek and sophisticated.

For the electric drivetrain, they wanted to use technology from a small company called AC Propulsion.

CAR PARTS: The chassis is the support frame of a car. The drivetrain connects the transmission to the axles, delivering power to the wheels.

Tesla's engineers and designers worked on the design of the body of the car. And of course all these components had to be fitted together, properly wired, and finished.

By the end of January 2005, Tesla had a prototype—built by a mere eighteen employees in six months.

During the next Tesla board meeting, Elon hopped behind the wheel of the test car. He wanted to show what the innovative technology could do and how it could feel in a sports car (as opposed to the decidedly not-a-sports-car feel of all electric cars that came before).

The board was impressed, and the team was able to get the additional funding to take the technology to the next level and make their first model: the Roadster. The board invested another $13 million into the company; Elon plopped down $9 million of that himself.

Later that summer the team discovered a major problem with the battery bricks. It happened at Martin Eberhard's July Fourth cookout. Somehow it came up in conversation—what happens if a strip of these batteries catches fire? So what do engineers at a cookout do when this kind of question arises? Why, they set them on fire, of course. So, bottom line: battery cells + heat = explosion.

Horrified, they realized they needed to find a way to keep those batteries cool.

> **WARNING!** Solving this problem involved many more experiments and explosions, but they solved it. Also, do not be tempted to amuse yourself by setting batteries on fire. It is extremely dangerous. Eventually, the Tesla engineers experimented in a blast area maintained by the fire department.

As Team Tesla chased down nothing less than the complete reimagining of electric cars, SpaceX was ready to launch the Falcon 1.

How Do You Solve a Problem Like Elon?

Elon's approach to problem-solving comes from his reading, training in physics, and engineering experience.

When Elon needed to figure out how to survive on his own in Canada, he relied on lessons learned from his all-time favorite book, *The Hitchhiker's Guide to the Galaxy.* A key theme in Douglas Adams's classic are the words "Don't panic."

It means when you encounter a problem, challenge, or obstacle, don't say, "Oh crap, I'm really in a pickle now." Instead say, "Here's a problem; how do I solve it?"

Remember, Elon first read this book while trying to determine the meaning of life. That's when the book taught him another lesson in problem-solving: You have to figure out the right question before you can attempt to answer it. Likewise, if you start with an answer, you still need to figure out the question.

Once Elon has the right question, he turns to an idea from physics called first principles. Using *first principles*, you boil down the problem to its most basic form. For example, how much money does it take for me to eat every day? Or what does it really cost to build a rocket?

And then you go where the problem-solving takes you, even into uncharted territory.

"It's rare that people try to think of something on a first principles basis," Elon explained. "They'll say, 'We'll do that because it's always been done that way.' Or they'll not do it because 'Well, nobody's ever done that, so it must not be good.' But that's just a ridiculous way to think. You have to build up the reasoning from the ground up—'from the first principles' is the phrase that's used in physics. You look at the fundamentals and construct your reasoning from that, and then you see if you have a conclusion that works or doesn't work, and it may or may not be different from what people have done in the past."[96]

CHAPTER 6

DON'T PANIC

The first rocket SpaceX built cost $6 million—a quarter of what similar rockets were going for, according to Elon.

That was the first win. Now he had to launch it, preferably without blowing it up in the process.

> Want to reach orbit? You'll have to travel at least 17,500 mph. The Apollo 10 mission flew at 24,989 mph to reach the moon!

In 2005, in the middle of the Pacific Ocean, some two thousand miles from Hawaii, Elon and his team took over a tiny speck of the Marshall Islands, called the Kwajalein Atoll—home to their launch site.

> How do you get a rocket to a tiny strip of coral reef in the middle of the Pacific? SpaceX used two options: a barge and, alternatively, a C-17 military transport plane.

At this point, Elon knew the rocket inside out—well enough, he said, to redraw the whole thing without the blueprints. It had taken two years longer than Elon originally hoped to get to this moment.

But the moment had arrived. It was time to show the world what SpaceX could do. Elon and Kimbal flew out together to witness the launch for themselves.

On November 26, 2005, at the launchpad, liquid oxygen filled the tanks. It was three o'clock in the morning. The team took up positions in mission control, some twenty-six miles away from the launch site.

The plan? First stage would launch and reach speeds of 6,850 mph. The rocket's second stage would then ignite and increase the speed to 17,000 mph.

LINGO ALERT! When you see a rocket on a launchpad, often you are looking at a multistage rocket. The rocket is made up of separate sections, each with its own engines and fuel, stacked one on top of the other or strapped to the sides of a central rocket. The sections are fired in stages and jettisoned (or discarded), lightening the load as the spacecraft climbs upward into orbit or beyond. It's not easy leaving Earth's gravity.

The six-hour launch window began. Preflight checks began. And then—the mission was aborted. They had a problem.

An oxygen tank valve was to blame. As the team worked to address that issue, others were discovered. A first launch would now be months away.

"I love deadlines. I love the whooshing sound they make as they go by,"[97] *Hitchhiker's Guide* author Douglas Adams once said. He was famous for *not* meeting them. And now Elon was too. Though to be fair, Elon set the impossible deadlines himself. This became known (mostly affectionately) as Elon time.

Falcon 1 small launch vehicle at Kwajalein Atoll. (Photo by Defense Advanced Research Projects Agency [DARPA].)

BACK IN THE SADDLE

MARCH 24, 2006—THE SOUND OF ELON'S FLIP-FLOPS smacking the floor set the rhythm as he paced back and forth in the Kwajalein control room. Falcon 1 was fueled and ready for launch. Preflight checks began. All systems were GO. The Merlin engine ignited. Falcon 1 roared skyward. A camera attached to the rocket recorded liftoff, climbing, climbing, and then . . . disaster. The rocket started to spin. A fire broke out above the engine. And now the whole business was falling back to Earth. It crashed onto the launchpad.

Air tanks on their backs and diving masks pulled into place, SpaceX employees fished rocket debris from the adjacent reef.

Elon reassured his team. "SpaceX is in this for the long haul and, come hell or high water, we are going to make this work,"[98] he said.

Even though the launch had not been successful, SpaceX had made enough progress that the company was in the running for a NASA contract to build a cargo ship to resupply the International Space Station. In August, NASA awarded SpaceX a $278 million contract to start development. This was a huge win for SpaceX. The development would lead to the Falcon 9 rocket and the Dragon capsule. But right now, SpaceX still needed to get its first rocket off the ground and into orbit successfully.

Meanwhile, at home, Justine and Elon welcomed triplets into the world. They now had a brood of five boys. Justine had published her first novel, *BloodAngel.* She was also detailing their often exciting private lives on her blog: Tales of lavish nightlife included cameos from the who's who of Hollywood like Leonardo DiCaprio. But under the surface, Elon and Justine's marriage was in trouble.

"Nevada's death sent me on a years-long inward spiral into depression and distraction,"[99] she recalled in an article she penned for *Marie Claire* magazine. In the same article, Justine made it clear that as their marriage unraveled, she felt like a trophy wife, no longer adored for her creative ambition, intellect, and accomplishments. Elon has never publicly discussed his side of what was going wrong, only that the relationship was "on the rocks."[100]

As Justine began talking to a therapist, Elon was under enormous pressure to get that rocket into orbit while Tesla needed to wow the world with a prototype.

SPLASH

ELON MAY *NOT* **HAVE BEEN RUNNING TESLA, BUT HE WAS VERY** involved in giving feedback on the car, its engineering, technology, and look. He also offered insight into the importance of how the car should be revealed to the public. He understood you only get one chance to make a splash.

Testing and tweaking, the team examined everything—aerodynamics, engine performance, design, battery cooling, and much more. Finally, a handful of prototypes were ready. The team prepared to introduce the world to a new era in electric cars.

In July 2006, the moment arrived. Tesla hosted a splashy event and promised a big announcement. VIPs like then-Governor Arnold Schwarzenegger attended, eager for a glimpse. The press was waiting. And when the Tesla Roadster was unveiled, they were not disappointed.

As Elon put it: "Until today, all electric cars have sucked."[101]

Elon Musk and Martin Eberhard presenting the Tesla Roadster, July 19, 2006.
(Photo by Glenn Koenig/Los Angeles Times via Getty Images.)

The headlines that followed were head spinners.

"The Tesla Roadster goes from zero to 60 in four noiseless seconds,"[102] crowed the *Washington Post*. *Wired* magazine simply showed a sleek black Roadster next to the heading: BATTERIES INCLUDED.

After the headlines, that old granola, low-budget reputation of electric cars had been turned on its head. It was now conceivable that you could have a crazy luxurious vehicle that also made a statement about the environment. The response was overwhelming.

Capturing the public's imagination, Tesla became something of an obsession. The media could not get enough. Celebrities and anyone else who could afford the roughly $100,000 Tesla Roadster were putting down deposits.

That said, showing off the car was exciting. Now the Tesla team just needed to produce and deliver them. Easy, right?

SUN

A MONTH AFTER THAT ANNOUNCEMENT, ELON WAS READY for another milestone—at yet another company. Remember that Rive-brothers-Burning-Man road trip? Their big idea had finally made a two-year-long journey from desert brainstorm through research and business plan to an actual *real live* company: SolarCity.

In August 2006, Peter and Lyndon Rive founded SolarCity with Elon as a financial investor. Owning a third of the company, he became the company's largest shareholder and chairman as well.

SOLARCITY: On December 13, 2012, Elon and Lyndon Rive's desert idea sparkled. SolarCity became a publicly traded company. The $8 a share initial public offering rose as high as 59 percent on its first day of trading.

Peter Rive, Elon Musk, Lyndon Rive, and NASDAQ's Bruce Aust at the SolarCity initial public offering. (Photo by Mark Von Holden/AP Images.)

Building off of Elon's original comments and questions, the Rive brothers began solving the challenge of getting solar panels on roofs. At the time, if you wanted to put solar panels on your house, you had to do a lot of the legwork yourself. You had to figure out how much energy your roof might produce, where to buy the panels, and then find someone who could stick them up. Plus, you had to pay for it all up-front. In short, it was a major commitment.

The Rives decided to streamline the entire process. SolarCity would analyze your solar power potential with their own software. Then, SolarCity would purchase the panels and install them. Customers would lease them over many years. Additional perks included being able to pass your lease on to a new homeowner should you sell your house.

They offered this service to businesses as well.

Between juggling SolarCity, Tesla, SpaceX, his admittedly rocky marriage, and fatherhood to five small boys, Elon had a *lot* going on. But he remained driven about the very things that excited him as a college student: the Internet, electric cars, space, and sustainable energy.

And he was determined to make a difference—through sheer force of will.

Gwynne Shotwell. (Photo by NASA/Kim Shiflett.)

NAME: Gwynne Shotwell, president, SpaceX

As a little girl, Gwynne Shotwell was full of questions such as, how does a car work? Gwynne's artist mom couldn't answer her third grader's questions, but ever supportive and encouraging, she gave Gwynne a book that could. As she delved into the mechanical and engineering details, Gwynne's interest grew.

And then there was a chance encounter that sealed her fate. Gwynne's mom took her to an event held by the Society of Women Engineers. Gwynne was enthralled by the engineer speaking to the crowd. The speaker wasn't just any engineer, but a *female* engineer. "I fell in love with the mechanical engineer that spoke," Gwynne explained during a TED Talk. "She was doing really critical work, and I loved her suit!"[103]

Gwynne decided right then and there that she too would be a mechanical engineer. And she did it: Her first job out of college was working as a mechanical engineer for Chrysler Motors.

Today Gwynne is the president of SpaceX. If you watch SpaceX's launches, you can often spy Gwynne jumping out of her chair when there is a successful launch!

TAKE AWAY THE ARMOR: What is it like to work for Elon for more than sixteen years? Gwynne spelled it out in her TED Talk. "He's funny, and fundamentally, without him saying anything, he drives you to do your best work. He doesn't have to say a word. You just want to do great work,"[104] she said, adding that she loves working with him.

CHAPTER 7

TYRANNY

On March 21, 2007, back on SpaceX's island outpost, Elon's attention was on Falcon 1. The next opportunity for launch had arrived.

Five, four, three, two, one, LIFTOFF!

Falcon 1 climbed high above the atoll. The first stage separated as scheduled. The second stage pushed the rocket onward. Then the top of the rocket separated. There was relief in the control room. Everything was going exactly as planned . . . until it wasn't.

The rocket suddenly broke apart and exploded. The launch was a failure.

Again SpaceX employees dissected the problem, found the cause, and worked under incredible pressure to correct it. That said, even with as much money as Elon brought to this effort, it was not an infinite supply. SpaceX needed a success and soon.

Not to mention Elon was spending an enormous amount of money at Tesla too. By now, around $100 million of his *own* money had burned up in these two companies. He needed a win.

WHEN IT RAINS IT POURS

BACK HOME IN CALIFORNIA, TESLA WAS IN TROUBLE. DELIV-ery of the world's unequivocally most mind-blowing electric car had been slated for 2006 ... which slid into 2007 ... which dragged into 2008.

Making a prototype is one thing. Building a car that can be driven for years and satisfy, even thrill, customers is another.

Problem after problem with engineering the Roadster cropped up. And now there was a transmission problem that was deemed insurmountable. Which meant the Tesla crew needed a fresh approach—or, in words that no one wants to hear after years of herculean effort—they needed to pretty much *start over*.

"We essentially had to do a complete reboot,"[105] Elon said. And that did not go unnoticed by one of the world's most important and trusted newspapers, the *New York Times*. Gossip in the industry and on blogs and auto websites centered on a rumor that customers would never get their Roadsters. This kind of coverage and talk only gave Tesla more to prove.

> How many lithium-ion batteries did it take to run the Roadster? 6,831

It did not help matters that by the end of 2007, the American economy had begun to unravel. Real estate values had plummeted, and people were struggling to keep their homes above water. Foreclosures skyrocketed, and credit began to dry up. The auto industry was hammered. After all, if you are struggling to keep a roof over your head, buying a new car is not an option. The Great Recession was underway.

As Tesla struggled to deliver the Roadster to the public, it went through management changes, and Elon became more and more involved in solving the big problems of the day—to the point of personally hopping on his jet and traveling across the world to buy a needed tool and deliver it to the factory floor. He was deep into the development of the battery packs, electronics, and transmission.

The media was having a field day with Tesla. One popular blog, *The Truth About Cars*, began a running entry called "Tesla Death Watch." Tesla's troubles were far from over. Elon went from media darling to media punching bag.

"It super sucked,"[106] he said.

> **ROADSTER'S CODE NAME:** DarkStar. It screamed from zero to 60 mph in 3.7 seconds. Until production of the Roadster ended in 2012, Tesla sold close to 2,500 Roadsters.

The Roadsters finally went into regular production in March 2008. But the original business plan was to build the Roadster in two years for $25 million. They were now four and half years into the process and approaching a cost of $140 million. Tesla's—and Elon's—troubles were far from over.

Tesla Roadster (© Tesla Motors Inc.).

While Elon was splitting his time between Los Angeles, Silicon Valley, and Kwajalein, his marital problems were only getting worse. In June 2008, Elon filed for divorce and shared custody of their boys. The divorce was widely reported in the media while Justine's blog covered her journey through what had become a pretty contentious fight. Anyone could log on and read all about it.

Elon never divulged his ultimate reason for ending it. As the lawyers worked out the details, Elon focused on his companies, his kids, and looking toward the future.

On a trip to London with a friend, the two men headed out to a club. Elon was not having a great time and wanted to leave. He'd only been there for ten minutes. But at that ten-minute mark, things took a dramatic change for the better. Someone introduced Elon to a twenty-two-year-old actress named Talulah Riley, who had appeared in the 2005 film *Pride & Prejudice*. She had never heard of Elon until that meeting. Elon and Talulah talked the night away. He showed her pictures of his rocket and the Roadster. "I remember thinking that this guy probably didn't get to talk to young actresses a lot and he seemed quite nervous,"[107] she said.

But he wasn't so nervous that he didn't ask her on a date. And the next night the two were together again for dinner. The day after that, the two met up for lunch. After Elon was back in the States, they kept up the romance over e-mail. Two weeks later, Talulah was on a plane to Los Angeles to visit Elon.

Five days after she set foot on U.S. soil, Elon proposed. To the shock of her parents, Talulah said yes to a man who was fourteen years older, going through a divorce, had five kids, and was running two impossibly challenging companies, and whom she now loved very much.

Meet the Musks

Elon Musk and Talulah Riley at the 2012 Environmental Awards.
(Photo by Kathy Hutchins / Shutterstock.com.)

NAME: Talulah Riley

DATE OF BIRTH: September 26, 1985

HOMETOWN: Hertfordshire, United Kingdom

Talulah Riley is an actor and author, appearing in the
HBO television series *Westworld* and in such films as
Thor: The Dark World (2013), *Inception* (2010), and
Pride & Prejudice (2005). Talulah's first novel, *Acts of
Love*, hit bookshelves in 2016, and she is working on
another.

THIRD TIME'S THE CHARM, RIGHT?

KWAJALEIN, MARSHALL ISLANDS, AUGUST 2, 2008—
The SpaceX island team gathered again for a third attempt to launch Falcon 1.

> **LINGO ALERT!** A spacecraft may have cargo or passengers aboard. Both are referred to as payload. The payload is what brings in money. Companies pay to put cargo aboard. Passengers pay for travel. Or in the case of astronauts, a government pays.

And this time they had paying customers. The payload included satellites from NASA and the U.S. Department of Defense. But they also had ashes on board. And not just any ashes. Falcon 1 carried the remains of 208 people, including astronaut Gordon Cooper and actor James Doohan, famous for his role as Scotty in the original *Star Trek* series, as in "Beam me up, Scotty." The ashes would be released in space.

T minus five. Four. Three. Two. One. Zero. ABORT. Yes, at T minus zero, the launch procedure came to a halt. Hours later, it was time to try again.

This time, the engines ignited and the rocket rushed toward orbit. Watching a webcast of the launch, the California team cheered at headquarters.

ROAD TRIP ALERT! SpaceX moves its headquarters to Hawthorne, California.

SpaceX headquarters, Hawthorne, California. (© SpaceX.)

Then the second stage did not fire. Silence and even tears swept over the SpaceX crowd. The third launch failed. The satellites were not deployed. The ashes would land in the ocean.

Elon put on a brave face for his team, but the consequences of a third failed launch were dire. They were running out of chances.

Developing the technology to go to space is not inexpensive. He had only enough money for one more launch.

And he wasn't the only one closely watching SpaceX's launches. The U.S. government was too. Elon knew that if the next launch was successful, SpaceX would be awarded extremely lucrative government contracts for putting satellites into space and more.

The pressure was on. Elon was determined that the fourth launch would work. If it didn't, Elon's space dream would end. The company would be finished. Failure may have been an option. Giving up was not.

ORBIT

KWAJALEIN, MARSHALL ISLANDS, SEPTEMBER 28, 2008—
Falcon 1 was ready for launch. The webcast began streaming. According to one employee, many of the SpaceX employees back at headquarters were trying not to vomit as the countdown approached liftoff. Elon watched from the control room. His brother was on hand as well.

Elon Musk watches the liftoff of the Falcon 1 spacecraft.
(Photo by Alex Coester/AP Images.)

Kimbal had been an early investor in SpaceX, which gave him a unique perspective. Years later when he and Elon gave an onstage interview together, he said, "The failures were spectacular. Seeing giant exploding rockets is quite an amazing sight!" As Elon sat uncomfortably, Kimbal laughed heartily and continued. "And I said,

'If all I get to do is see these rockets explode, it is well worth every dime I put into this company!"[108]

Elon's pal and old college housemate Adeo knew that if this launch failed, Elon was destined to become a business school case study on failure.

"Everything hinged on that launch," he said. "This was more than his fortune at stake—it was his credibility."[109]

Elon watched the engines ignite and flames rush out of the Merlin engine, sending Falcon 1 off the launchpad. Everyone cheered. First stage separation? Check! Second stage ignition? Check! Fairing release? Check!

And finally, like a dream, the Falcon 1 reached orbit. Mission accomplished!

Successful launch of Falcon 1, September 2008. (© SpaceX.)

"When the launch was successful," Kimbal said, "everyone burst into tears. It was one of the most emotional experiences I've had."[110]

Elon walked out of the control room to address his now-500-person staff. "There are a lot of people who thought we couldn't do it—a lot actually—but as the saying goes, 'the fourth time is the charm,' right?"[111]

And then Elon put the world on notice. This was the first step of many to come.

BOOKSHELF! *Benjamin Franklin* by Walter Isaacson

Why Elon loves it: "[Benjamin Franklin] was an entrepreneur and sort of started from nothing, actually just like a runaway kid." Franklin built his printing business and pursued other interests in science and politics, becoming one of America's Founding Fathers. "He is one of the people I most admire,"[112] Elon said. "Franklin's pretty awesome."

BUT WAIT, THERE'S MORE

ELON MAY HAVE HAD A SUCCESSFUL LAUNCH UNDER HIS BELT, but that did not magically put money in the coffers. SpaceX was positioned to grow and attract more customers. But this doesn't happen overnight, and there were employees to pay.

Over at Tesla, money was running out so quickly that drastic measures had to be taken. Elon committed all his cash reserves, took over as CEO, and announced layoffs in October.

He was determined to see his companies through this economic downturn.

"It's like if you have two kids. What do you do? Do you spend all of your money to maximize the probability of success of one? Or do you try to keep both alive?"[113] Elon explained.

It was a huge risk as *everything* in his life seemed to be falling apart. Justine had learned about this engagement to Talulah. It went over like a lead balloon.

"There were always all these negative articles about Tesla, and the stories about SpaceX's third failure. It hurt really bad. You have these huge doubts that your life is not working, your car is not working, you're going through a divorce and all of those things,"[114] he told biographer Ashlee Vance. "I didn't think we would overcome it." In fact, he thought they were doomed.

By December, Tesla was on the brink of bankruptcy.

Tesla employees offered what they had to invest, as did Kimbal, and Elon's friends, including Google cofounder Sergey Brin—all were trying to keep Tesla alive.

Elon was trying to keep his fundamental mission alive: nothing less than saving the planet. His answer to avoid pumping Earth's limited oil supply out of the ground was Tesla. And Tesla's very survival seemed like little more than a minute-by-minute gamble. Elon's answer to dodging a planetary catastrophe was SpaceX. That, too, was in doubt. Nearly everything that Elon cared about was in jeopardy.

"This wasn't Elon facing adversity," Kimbal explained to *Esquire*. "Personal bankruptcy was a daily conversation. Tesla was on the limb to deliver cars that people already paid for. Bankruptcy would have been easier than what he did. He threw everything he had into keeping Tesla alive."[115] Anybody else would have given up.

And in his spare time, nasty divorce proceedings had put his family life in a tough spot and a very public one as well. Elon and Talulah decided to retreat to Boulder, Colorado, to spend the holidays with Kimbal and his family.

Then, just two days before Christmas, NASA awarded SpaceX a contract worth $1.6 billion. Billion.

The next day, on Christmas Eve, Tesla closed on a new round of venture capital funding that would keep the company afloat.

Venture capital is funding for start-ups from investors who see potential for long-term growth. It can come from individual angel investors, investment banks, or venture capital firms. Venture capital firms typically invest larger sums of money than angel investors. Because start-ups are so risky, most firms do a ton of research, called due diligence, before investing. They look at the business model, what has been done so far, what type of market exists for your product, and more—all to understand what they are putting their money into. In exchange for their investment, venture capital firms will receive large chunks of equity in the start-up and will want a say in big decisions. Sometimes they even offer input on how the company should be run.

Elon burst into tears. And then it hit him. Christmas. Talulah. Gift. Elon Musk—the famed inventor, disruptor, and visionary—had been so busy trying to rescue his companies from certain doom that he had not even bought his new fiancée a Christmas present.

Running down the street, searching for a place to buy her a gift, his only option was not awesome. A trinket store. "They were about to close," he said. "The best thing I could find were plastic monkeys with coconuts—those 'hear no evil, see no evil' monkeys."[116]

As the global economic crisis continued to unfold, both General Motors and Chrysler filed for bankruptcy in 2009 and the U.S. government spent nearly $80 billion to bail out the auto industry. But Tesla, the Silicon Valley automobile start-up that should never have gotten off the ground in the first place, survived the Great Recession.

Car, Drive Me Home!

Today, all new Teslas come with autopilot hardware. As the company puts it, "All Tesla vehicles produced in our factory, including Model 3, have the hardware needed for full self-driving capability at a safety level substantially greater than that of a human driver."[117]

Tesla customers can buy, or their model may come way with, various levels of autopilot *software*. One was to think of it is like an in-app purchase. While full self-driving is not yet available, the car can do a lot to help drivers negotiate traffic, avoid accidents, and get on and off the highway safely.

Using a suite of cameras, ultrasonic sensors, and radar, the autopilot monitors detect what's around the car. An onboard computer processes that information with an AI assist. Tesla also offers an enhanced autopilot for lane changes, matching speed to driving conditions, exiting highways, side collision warning, emergency braking, front collision warning, and other fun features like summoning the car to pick you up. Car parked in a tight garage space? Tap the summon button and the car can drive itself out of that spot and you can hop in and be on your way. But autopilot also comes with a clear warning: The driver must pay attention and be prepared to react and take over as needed. Tesla also has plans to roll out fully self-driving autopilot.

CHAPTER 8

THE WHEEL, REINVENTED

While Elon guided SpaceX and Tesla through those tricky years, Tesla had also been working on plans for a new model: the Model S.

THE MODEL S PRICE TAG: $78,000.

In that awful year, 2008, there was a bright spot. Elon had hired the best car designer he could find: a man named Franz von Holzhausen.

Franz von Holzhausen (front) with Elon Musk. (Photo by Jurvetson.)

As a kid, Franz filled his notebooks and drawing paper with sketches of cars. As an adult, he helped reimagine Volkswagen's iconic Beetle. The original debuted in 1939, and reached peak popularity in the 1960s. The New Beetle launched in 1997 and took the U.S. market by storm—the car was a surprise megahit. After nearly eight years at VW, Franz's career took him to General Motors and then to Mazda. Along the way, he began taking green materials into account when designing cars.

Now, Franz could focus his clear talent and experience on designing the Model S. The car needed to stand out. He settled on a look that was futuristic but still accessible, something you'd want to be seen driving *and* could still haul you and your stuff from place to place.

Working in a tent in a corner of the SpaceX factory, Franz and his team began work. In just three months, they had a workable design, and a prototype began to take shape. Inspired by the feel of the greatest sports cars in the world but also the demands of family life—let's face it, a two-seater means a family of four will face an impossible choice of whom to strap to the roof—the Model S was well underway.

LINGO ALERT! The code name for the Model S was WhiteStar.

Meeting with Franz and the design team every Friday, Elon pored over every detail, "every nuance of the car. Every bumper, every curve, every little tiny piece of the car. What's right. What's wrong. And then that has to be filtered against the engineering needs, the ergonomic needs, regulatory requirements,"[118] he explained. He believed you had to care about every millimeter in order to produce a "good product." Translation, they were shooting for nothing less than perfect.

In spring 2009, the press and invited guests walked into SpaceX headquarters. With a factory backdrop worthy of Tony Stark, the Model S was on proud display. It was the first luxury all-electric sedan. The car was not anywhere close to complete, but again, Elon succeeded in wowing the media and reengaging the public in a now familiar plot line: Elon was molding the impossible into reality. As with the Roadster, orders of the Model S poured in.

Tesla Model S. (Photo by Tesla Motors, Inc.)

And other car makers noticed Tesla's technology. Daimler, maker of Mercedes, ordered four thousand Tesla battery packs that it took back to Germany to install in its cars. Then Tesla provided batteries for Daimler's Smart car.

"Coils of aluminum and plastic pellets come in and cars come out,"[119] Elon explained to journalist Sarah Lacy, who covers the start-up world. "We do real hard-core manufacturing. We do all the vehicle engineering, all the power train engineering, all the software, and we also of course do all the styling and design of the car."[120]

Almost a year after that flashy press event, Tesla received an enormous loan from the U.S. government to keep making electric batteries and to build electric vehicles in the United States. The green energy loan was for $465 million.

Tesla quickly scooped up a car factory. In 2010, after the Great Recession had taken its toll, you could get a car factory for quite a bargain. Plunking down $42 million for a 5.3-million-square-foot facility, Tesla now had a place to make the Model S.

Okay, $42 million doesn't exactly sound like pocket change, but that being said, the factory, previously owned by both Toyota *and* GM, was once worth a billion dollars. Suddenly $42 million doesn't seem like a lot.

> **ROAD TRIP ALERT!** Tesla's factory is located at 45500 Fremont Boulevard in Fremont, California. Tesla headquarters moved to 3500 Deer Creek Road, Palo Alto.

It was another important step in solving the world's oil problem. The plan was for the Roadster to pay for the Model S, which would pay for the Model X, which would pay for a car the masses could afford—in the same way that televisions and smartphones always work. The first model comes out and is usually out of reach for most. But as more models come out with time, the price comes down.

PUBLIC

ON JUNE 29, 2010, IN NEW YORK CITY, TESLA WAS ABOUT TO hit a milestone: becoming a publicly traded company. Elon took his place above the trading floor. Talulah stood next to him smiling. Each held one of his boys on their hip. Other members of Tesla's team crowded in with them.

Elon Musk celebrates Tesla's initial public offering at the NASDAQ opening bell on June 29, 2010. (Photo by Mark Lennihan/AP Images.)

The crowd screamed as Elon rang the opening bell at NASDAQ. Only eighteen months earlier, Tesla had been on the verge of collapse. And now? Elon and the members of Team Tesla clapped, smiled, waved their arms, and shouted in celebration. Tesla was officially a publicly traded company. The stock offered at $17 a share.

Tesla became the first American car company to go public since Ford in 1956.

The reasons to celebrate did not stop there. Later that year, in September, private planes and helicopters dropped off wedding guests in a small town in the Scottish Highlands. Gathering at a stone cathedral built in the thirteenth century, guests waited for the arrival of the bride and groom. Elon and Talulah did not disappoint, pulling up in a white Rolls-Royce. The couple exchanged vows, and just like a fairy tale, they left in a horse-drawn carriage and danced the night away in a nearby castle. Elon and Talulah were finally husband and wife.

After Tesla reported its first quarterly profit, the stock price hit $130 a share in July 2013. In 2018, Tesla's stock price even soared as high as $383 a share.

Back in Silicon Valley, the team at Tesla threw themselves into car development. And Elon was not easy to please. Once the prototypes were made, he would drive them, sometimes for an entire weekend, then return the car with a list of changes that needed to be made.

"Tesla is a hard-core technology company. We do really serious engineering. The only bulk value in a company is if you are doing hard work to solve tough problems,"[121] Elon explained. He wanted Tesla's cars to be nothing less than, well, perfect. Period.

BOOKSHELF! *Einstein: His Life and Universe* by Walter Isaacson chronicles the unlikely path and amazing contributions of Albert Einstein, a book that Elon learned a lot from.

IT'S COMPLICATED

REMEMBER WHEN ELON DISCOVERED THAT THE PRICE OF rockets was overly inflated? He made a similar discovery about the parts used to make rockets. They were way overpriced. Elon found that irritating. If something cost pennies to make, it shouldn't cost thousands of dollars to buy. What does Elon do in such a situation? Makes the parts himself.

So SpaceX began manufacturing its own. And just like Tesla would not simply assemble a bunch of parts from somewhere else into a car at the Tesla factory, neither would SpaceX. The rocket company would make as many of the parts as it could, which would continue to bring the cost of getting to space down.

It's hard to overstate just how much this approach broke new ground. It was that same attitude Elon had always had of not going along with the status quo, always questioning why thing are the way they are. And if there wasn't a good answer to that question, he looked for a new way.

This level of extreme innovation took tremendous intellectual and physical energy. And that often bumped up against a harsh reality: There are only twenty-four hours in a day. And in theory, you are supposed to sleep for some portion of that.

Elon tried to get six hours of sleep a night. Attached to his smartphone, he could read and reply to e-mail from both SpaceX and Tesla—whether being chauffeured to the office, lying in bed, or sitting in the bathroom.

Having shared custody of his kids often meant bringing them along to work events.

"They're remarkably unimpressed,"[122] he said.

After ringing in 2012, a single tweet turned the spotlight back on Elon's personal life. "@rileytalulah It was an amazing four years. I will love you forever. You will make someone very happy one day."[123]

Elon and Talulah separated. In an interview with *Forbes* magazine, Elon admitted he had simply fallen out of love with Talulah. They had been living apart for six months.

"We took some time apart for several months to see if absence makes the heart grow fonder, and unfortunately it did not," he continued. "I still love her, but I'm not in love with her. And I can't really give her what she wants."[124] Unlike Justine, Talulah was not publicly discussing the breakup, and she and Elon were still very close friends.

Next, it was Tesla's turn to garner international attention. In February 2012, the governor of California, Jerry Brown, stood in the center of a stage in Los Angeles. Brown's voice echoed as he gushed about California's special culture of innovation and talent for great design. The crowd cheered, ready for the main event.

Introduced as the person who "pushes the ideal that nothing is impossible,"[125] Elon took the stage.

"We created Tesla to make a difference in the world. The world desperately needs sustainable transport," he said to the audience. "So the thing is, if you don't make compelling electric cars, if you don't make electric cars that are—not almost as good as gasoline cars, not as good as gasoline cars—but if you don't make electric cars that are *better*, then it's not going to happen."

TURN UP THE VOLUME! When you are ready to blast your favorite playlist while driving a Tesla, the volume goes to eleven. The number was picked as a reference to the classic movie *This Is Spinal Tap.*

On the stage, he was at ease, making his case, working the room, selling his vision. Whether painting a grand vision for the bigger picture of Tesla's mission or delving into technical detail, his delivery developed a special Elon signature, a combination of confidence, technical knowledge, and unbridled enthusiasm. The performance was a far cry from the school days when he was tormented by bullies and struggled to make friends.

In April 2012, Elon Musk joined some of the wealthiest people in the world and signed the Giving Pledge, a commitment to use most of your wealth for giving back. The idea started two years earlier when a group of forty billionaire philanthropists, led by Bill and Melinda Gates and Warren Buffet, decided to inspire the ultrarich to give more, give sooner, and give smarter. More than 183 of the world's wealthiest individuals and couples have signed the pledge.

"What if you could have a car that has more functionality than a minivan, more style than an SUV, and more performance than a sports car?" Elon asked the crowd, pausing. "That's the Model X!"

Cue the dance club music and lighting. Franz drove the Model X onto the stage with six of the car's engineers and designers piled inside. And when they were ready to step out, the doors *lifted* open— like batwings.

Tesla Model X. (Photo by Tesla Motors Inc.)

Okay, technically they are called falcon wings. Whatever you want to call them, they were a showstopper. Sure, the Model S hadn't been delivered yet. But it didn't seem to matter much. Customers were fans, and they were willing to wait.

> Going from zero to sixty in 2.9 seconds, the Model X can seat seven adults in three rows of seats. There's storage behind the third row and what Elon calls a "frunk," trunk space under the hood of the car—because there isn't a gas engine taking up that space. Deliveries began in 2015.

CHARGED

THAT SUMMER OF 2012, ELON CIRCLED A MODEL S, CROUCH-
ing down, opening the doors, and taking a long, careful inventory of
every detail. The men and women who built the car looked on with
pride, teary eyed.

After inspecting each car, Elon handed them over to their new
owners—confident in the quality, craftsmanship, and design.

It was an emotional moment of triumph, captured by the media
and cheered by invited guests. Delays meant that delivery of the first
Model S cars was at least a year and a half late, but it still happened.
Those first owners drove their sedans home. Elon and his team had
delivered on a promise that most car experts had thought was impossible. He was late but he did it.

DOUBTERS, AKA SHORT SELLERS. There are investors
who buy stock because they think the share price will rise,
making them money. And there are short sellers who bet that the
stock price will drop. Short sellers were putting huge wagers on
Tesla's future doom.

In the fall, Elon expanded Tesla's business. Now it wasn't just
making cars, it was charging them too. Remember, Elon wanted Tesla
to replace traditional gas-powered cars, so they not only needed to
look good, they needed to handle everything traditional cars could—
including long distances.

Three hundred miles on a single charge was certainly a game
changer—unless you needed to drive across the country or even from

Los Angeles to San Francisco. To solve this issue, Tesla decided to make charging stations for their cars. They started with six stations in California as far north as Sacramento, where Tesla owners could plug in midtrip and recharge with just a thirty-minute stop. And it was free. As of this writing, there are more than 1,300 Supercharger stations throughout North America, Asia, Europe, and the Middle East. Tesla also offered turn-by-turn directions for drivers, complete with en-route charging station locations.

As more Teslas hit the road, Tesla began a transition in 2017 from free Supercharger use for life to pay per use. Now buyers new to Tesla receive a credit for some free charging every year, which amounts to about a thousand miles of range. Once the credit is exhausted in a year, they pay a small fee for each charge. It still generally works out to be cheaper than gas. Tesla uses the revenue to maintain and expand the charging stations. That said, Tesla sometimes offers supercharging for life as part of various promotions.

Tesla Supercharger stations in Rochester, New York.

All that triumph and expansion seemed an unlikely buildup to a moment of national humiliation. But everyone across the United States and around the world who tuned to watch the presidential debate between Barack Obama and Governor Mitt Romney was in for a surprise. Tesla was about to make a cameo—as a loser.

Remember that loan from the U.S. government? Well, in a charged exchange, Romney brought up Obama's green energy loans. Tesla wasn't the only company who received one. So did a handful of other green energy companies, some of which had gone bankrupt.

Romney spouted at Obama, "But don't forget, you put $90 billion, like fifty years' worth of breaks, into—into solar and wind, to Solyndra and Fisker and Tesla and Ener1. I mean, I had a friend who said you don't just pick the winners and losers, you pick the losers, all right? So this—this is not—this is not the kind of policy you want to have if you want to get America energy secure."[126]

So at a moment when the world was watching, Tesla was branded a loser. Yikes. The media seized on the exchange. A month later, Romney had lost the election.

And by the next spring, Elon went on national television to reveal the final tally. Tesla had just repaid that loan in full—*nine* years ahead of schedule[127] and *with* interest.

"Ultimately, the U.S. taxpayers actually made a profit of over twenty million dollars on this loan,"[128] he told Bloomberg Television.

Elon loved paying back that loan. It proved his naysayers dead wrong.

What Do You Do When You Are Out of Batteries?

Tesla Gigafactory in Sparks, Nevada. (Photo by Tesla Motors Inc.)

Tesla's demand for lithium-ion batteries quickly outran the world's supply.

Not having the batteries on time delayed car production.

In 2014, Elon found himself back in the desert, looking for the right spot to build a factory—where Tesla could make its own batteries.

Meet the Gigafactory, located in, um . . . Sparks, Nevada, on Electric Avenue.

The $5 billion factory is designed to be built in phases, but once complete, the total size will be 5.8 million square feet. How big is that? Big enough to fit more than two hundred White Houses inside.

In a TED Talk, Elon was asked how many Gigafactories it would take to get us to a future where we don't need to feel guilty about energy use. That means enough lithium-ion batteries to run everything that's currently powered by fossil fuels in the world. Without flinching, Elon said, "It's about a hundred roughly. It's not ten or a thousand. Most likely a hundred."[129] As of 2018, there are plans to build Gigafactories in China and Europe.

CHAPTER 9

OF COURSE I STILL LOVE YOU

In the summer of 2013, Elon dressed up in a medieval costume to get ready for his third wedding. Soon he was gazing at his bride-to-be, clad in a medieval-inspired silk gown with bejeweled accents and matching headdress. Talulah and Elon were making a second trip to the altar.

In their time apart, Talulah had been busy acting in various movies and writing a screenplay for another. She and Elon had kept up a friendship after their divorce. A friendship that once again turned romantic. Now back in Los Angeles as Mrs. Musk, she would attempt to juggle writing, acting, and helping to raise her five stepsons.

Elon was still working long hours, managing two companies, serving on the board of SolarCity, and sorting through the constant explosion of ideas in his head. Often, he would spend hours awake in the middle of the night, pacing, working through ideas, sketching them out or e-mailing himself.

Describing his schedule at the time, he said, "I'll be working at SpaceX on Monday. And then Monday night flight to the Bay Area. Tuesday and Wednesday at Tesla. Fly back Wednesday night. Spend Thursday and Friday at SpaceX."[130] And on the weekends? He was at the airport again first thing Saturday morning to spend the day at Tesla . . . and then back to Los Angeles to spend Sunday at SpaceX. It was a lot, but in Elon's world, there was no time to rest.

In fact, that August, just a month after the wedding, Elon was announcing a new idea for getting around the planet, as he put it, a fifth mode of transportation: the hyperloop.

Think bullet train, but crash proof, weatherproof, and much, *much* faster. He felt sure you could take a hyperloop from downtown Los Angeles to downtown San Francisco in thirty minutes.

As he started talking about the idea in interviews, people would sometimes ask if he was serious. It seemed outlandish.

Elon *was* serious. Only, he couldn't possibly fit that in. And yet the idea had the potential to help him reach his ultimate goal of getting humans off of gasoline, an effort that couldn't wait.

So instead of starting another company to chase that down, he published a public paper on the idea, spelling out what he thought was possible—with the hope that others in the tech community would pick up the idea and run with it. And they did. A start-up called Hyperloop One quickly set to work developing high-speed vacuum tunnel travel, eventually building a test site in Nevada. Another group of entrepreneurs and engineers started a company called Hyperloop Transportation Technologies.

You can read Elon's original paper here: www.spacex.com/sites/spacex/files/hyperloop_alpha.pdf

And it wasn't like Elon did not have enough to work on. SpaceX had already figured out how to launch rockets into orbit. Since 2012 it had made six deliveries to the International Space Station for NASA, using the larger Falcon 9 rocket and the Dragon cargo capsule. The company was also regularly putting satellites into orbit with Falcon 9.

But in the desert, there was something else Elon wanted to master—*landing* a rocket. Nothing could reduce the cost of going to space more than figuring out how to reuse those rockets. And that meant the boosters would need to return to Earth and gently settle onto terra firma. Regular testing was underway. How could you bring a rocket back to Earth, slow it down, and land it upright?

SpaceX would also need a way to land over water. Elon's answer to that was a drone ship, a remote-controlled landing pad. SpaceX needed two. The Atlantic would be covered by a drone ship named *Just Read the Instructions* and the Pacific by *Of Course I Still Love You.*

Just Read the Instructions drone ship. (© SpaceX.)

But to even set down a rocket safely on land, well, one SpaceX commentator described the problem like this: "Launching a pencil over the Empire State Building, having it reverse, come back down and land on a shoebox on the ground during a windstorm."[131] Oh, just that.

BOOKSHELF! *The Player of Games* by Iain M. Banks, a science fiction novel published in 1988, part of his Culture series. This book is set in a world that happens to have high-speed vacuum trains, human and machine symbiosis . . . oh, and two spaceships named *Of Course I Still Love You* and *Just Read the Instructions*. In 2018, Elon announced that a third drone ship under construction would be called *A Shortfall of Gravitas*, also inspired by the Culture series.

STICK THE LANDING

MONDAY, DECEMBER 21, 2015

8:29 p.m. (EST)

Cape Canaveral, Florida.

SpaceX Cape Canaveral Launch Control. (© SpaceX.)

T minus twenty seconds.

Under a clear night sky at Launch Complex 40, the control room's countdown commands blared from loudspeakers. Elon stood behind his team of rocket scientists, engineers, and experts as they hunched over their computers. On the screens in front of them was a *live* video feed of the Falcon 9 rocket sitting on its launchpad.

T minus ten. Nine. Eight. Seven.

Everything had to be perfect for launch. Everything was on the line. Just six months earlier, the last rocket launch ended in spectacular failure: an explosion.

Now, here they were again.

FALCON 9 SPECS

ROCKET STAGES: Two

HEIGHT: 229 feet

DIAMETER: 12 feet

ENGINES: 9 Merlin engines

Six. Five. "Go for launch."

SpaceX was seconds away from trying to make rocket history. The goal? Launch a rocket into orbit, deploy satellites, and then *land* the rocket booster back on Earth so it could be reused—a feat that had never been done before.

Most rockets—rockets that take millions of dollars to design, build, and successfully launch—are actually nothing but . . . future trash. Each rocket can only be used once. It goes like this. The rocket blasts off. The rocket boosters separate from the payload in stages as it soars through the sky. Some fall back to Earth and land in the ocean. Others remain in orbit, contributing to millions of pieces of useless and potentially dangerous debris orbiting the Earth. Not really a great plan, but there was no other choice.

Need to know everything about Falcon 9? Fear not, it has a user's guide: www.spacex.com/sites/spacex/files/falcon_9_users_guide_rev_2.0.pdf

The technology for a reusable orbital rocket did not exist. Until now . . . hopefully.

Across the country at SpaceX headquarters in Hawthorne, California, a crowd gathered. They suddenly fell silent, watching every move in Cape Canaveral on a giant screen.

Four. Three. Two. One.

Falcon 9's engines roared. In a cloud of dust and smoke, the blazing rocket blasted off the launchpad.

"We have liftoff."

Falcon 9 thundered skyward.

Elon made his way toward the exit. Breathless and running, he raced outside to watch it fly.

Looking up, he saw Falcon 9's fiery glow become smaller and smaller as it flew out of sight.

The sky was black. Now he had to wait. Would the booster separate and return to Earth?

Elon listened to mission control through outdoor speakers as he waited. He searched the sky for a glimmer of the returning rocket.

He wasn't the only one feeling nervous. The crowd back in California stood quiet with clasped hands. Some covered their mouths. Tortured looks spread across many of their faces.

Employees watch launch from SpaceX headquarters. (© SpaceX.)

Then, above Cape Canaveral, a sonic boom filled the sky. The rocket was on its way back to Earth.

FALCON 9

DISTANCE TO ORBIT: **398 miles**

TILT: **47 degrees**

Suddenly a bright light appeared in the distance and grew bigger, closer to Earth.

Would history be made this time? Could they land the rocket? The rocket's booster blazed, slowing it down as it zoomed toward the launchpad. Suddenly out of a stream of fire, the landing legs deployed.

"The Falcon has landed."

Falcon 9 First Stage landing. (© SpaceX.)

ROAD TRIP ALERT! Installed in April 2016, that first returned booster is on permanent display at SpaceX headquarters in Hawthorne.

Mission control erupted. Gwynne shot out of her seat. Employees hugged each other, jumped up and down, and screamed for a long time, finally chanting, "USA! USA! USA!" And fresh on their minds was the fact that the leading space experts of the world, just a few years ago, did not think SpaceX could do what it set out to do.

Today the company has an explosion blooper reel for your enjoyment. youtu.be/bvim4rsNHkQ

The space industry had changed. History had been made. By a company started by an Internet Guy who was reading about rocketry just thirteen years earlier.

"It's a revolutionary moment. No one has ever brought a booster, an orbital-class booster, back intact,"[132] Elon told reporters. They had done it. Revolutionized space travel. Accomplished the impossible, and opened up the heavens in a way that had never been done before.

SpaceX landed a booster on a barge floating in the ocean in 2016, and it launched a *preflown* booster into orbit for the first time in March 2017.

ALL PART OF THE MASTER PLAN

SO IMAGINE DRIVING YOUR TESLA HOME AFTER A BUSY DAY. You park it in the garage, plug it into the wall to keep it nice and charged. Only, the charge isn't coming from the electric company. Instead it's coming from the solar tiles on your roof and stored right there at your house. And what if Tesla provided all of that, the wall charger, the battery storage, and the solar cells on your roof. That full-circle vision was very much on Elon's mind and had been for quite some time.

In 2016 Tesla moved toward this vision by acquiring SolarCity. SolarCity had become the solar industry's largest installer. By now SolarCity had installed panels on more than forty-five thousand buildings. Its customer base was exploding.

It had all been a part of Elon's master plan—for at least ten years, published on Tesla's website. The last paragraph of the plan got right down to the bottom line:

Build sports car.

Use that money to build an affordable car.

Use *that* money to build an even more affordable car.

While doing above, also provide zero emission electric power generation options.

Don't tell anyone.

LINGO ALERT! Tesla's Powerwall is a battery for homes that have solar panels on the roof. The solar cells capture the energy and send it to the Powerwall for storage and consumption.

Tesla Powerwall. (Photo by Tesla Motors Inc.)

Not everyone was as thrilled about the deal as Elon and his cousins. Critics were quick to point out that SolarCity went into debt to fuel its growth. Others pointed out that founders Lyndon and Peter had laid off staff and cut their own salaries to just a dollar a year each. To some, it looked like a bailout.

But the deal proceeded and was approved by Tesla's shareholders. Lyndon and Peter stayed on until the deal closed and then both left the company. Lyndon said he was in search of his next start-up. Peter, too, began to explore what was next for him.

These weren't the only good-byes. In the fall of 2016, Elon and Talulah's second marriage to each other ended in divorce, but with the couple vowing they would always love each other and would stay close friends.

As Elon made his way through divorce proceedings, enduring enormous public interest in his private life, he began spending time with someone who was also going through a very public divorce: actress and humanitarian Amber Heard. She was in the midst of finalizing her divorce from actor Johnny Depp.

The next spring, Amber announced to the world that she and Elon were dating by planting a red kiss on his cheek, snapping a picture, and posting it on Instagram.

Amber Heard's Instagram post (screenshot taken October 29, 2018).

Elon had fallen deeply in love.

Paparazzi captured every shot they could—Amber with Elon's jacket draped across her shoulders with him all smiles beside her, a street-side kiss, Amber and Elon on the red carpet. Even the couple themselves shared fun-loving shots taken with Elon's boys on a vacation in Australia. As their relationship passed the one-year mark, Elon was ramping up to launch Tesla's Model 3.

Standing offstage on July 29, 2017, Elon was about to head out in front of the crowd and the white-hot light of the international media to launch the car for the masses. It was an achievement Tesla had been working toward since its inception.

And yet Elon was having a hard time pulling it together. He needed to knock his presentation out of the park. His showmanship was an essential ingredient in big Tesla moments. But, the fact was, Elon was heartbroken. Amber had broken it off just three days before.

"It took every ounce of will to be able to do the Model 3 event and not look like the most depressed guy around,"[133] he later told *Rolling Stone*'s Neil Strauss.

But then, he thought about the people depending on him. He tried to meditate, drank a couple of Red Bulls, cranked the music and rallied.

Talking to *Rolling Stone*, he didn't hold back in describing the depth of his misery and loneliness. "When I was a child, there's one thing I said, 'I never want to be alone.' That's what I would say. I don't want to be alone."[134]

It was the loneliness that got to him. "I will never be happy without having someone," he said. "Going to sleep alone kills me. It's like I don't know what that feels like: Being in a big empty house, and the footsteps echoing through the hallway, no one there—and no one on the pillow next to you."[135]

Maria

Puerto Rico, September 20, 2017—Swirling in the Atlantic, Hurricane Maria grew into a monster. Sustained winds hit 155 mph as the Category 4 storm barreled across Puerto Rico. Entire trees were ripped out of the ground. A wall of water rushed inland, with a force capable of unthinkable destruction. The screaming storm peeled away roofs.

And then everything went black. Power lines flew away with the wind. Power poles snapped, and giant waves carried them out to sea. The power infrastructure was devastated, and the island plunged into darkness.

Debris filled the streets. A few days after the storm left a stricken island in its wake, the enormity of the situation began to sink in. Puerto Rico had sustained the kind of damage that could not be easily fixed. No one had a quick solution for getting the power back on. And that affected people's houses, their ability to use their cell phones, hospitals' power supplies, and schools' power supplies.

The images coming out of Puerto Rico were shocking. It looked like a war-torn country.

A couple of weeks later, most of Puerto Rico still had no power. The island's governor reached out to Elon directly over Twitter, asking for help.

Ricardo Rossello ✓
@ricardorossello

Follow ⌄

@elonMusk Let's talk. Do you want to show the world the power and scalability of your #TeslaTechnologies? PR could be that flagship project.

> **Elon Musk** ✓ @elonmusk
> Replying to @stapf
>
> The Tesla team has done this for many smaller islands around the world, but there is no scalability limit, so it can be done for Puerto Rico too. Such a decision would be in the hands of the PR govt, PUC, any commercial stakeholders and, most importantly, the people of PR.

5:34 PM - 5 Oct 2017

5,187 Retweets **10,314** Likes

💬 677   ↻ 5.2K   ♡ 10K

Elon Musk ✓ @elonmusk · 6 Oct 2017   ⌄
Replying to @ricardorossello
I would be happy to talk. Hopefully, Tesla can be helpful.

💬 265   ↻ 1.3K   ♡ 5.6K

*Twitter conversation between Ricardo Rosselló and Elon Musk
(screenshot taken October 2018).*

Elon's teams at Tesla and SolarCity sprang into action. Just two weeks later, a month after the storm struck, Tesla restored power to the island's children's hospital. They installed solar panels, batteries, and infrastructure, creating a self-sufficient microgrid.

WHAT'S A MICROGRID? Well, first think about what happens in blackouts. When something disrupts the power grid, an entire region of the United States can be plunged into darkness for days.

That's because we are all connected to the same large power grid. And when equipment fails or huge lines come down, trouble travels farther along the line. But if you make smaller grids, or microgrids (say your neighborhood's connected on the same solar-based grid), if one microgrid experiences an issue, the impact of the outage is far smaller. That's because it's a smaller network that can function independently of a larger regional grid.

Then Tesla began restoring power to a senior housing center, followed by a sewer treatment plant.

Homeowners in Puerto Rico who already had solar panels were offered the chance to buy Tesla's Powerwall batteries while Tesla was on hand to install them. Solar energy could be stored overnight, which would mean independence from Puerto Rico's downed power grid and freedom from generators.

As the 2018 hurricane season approached with many on the island still without power, Elon announced that Tesla had eleven thousand energy storage projects underway in Puerto Rico.

LINGO ALERT! Tesla's Powerpack is a "fully integrated, AC-connected energy storage system with everything needed to connect to a building or utility network." While the Powerwall handles energy storage for a home, Tesla designed a larger battery system called the Powerpack for businesses and utilities to create their own microgrids. Powerpack stores energy from the power grid, or from on-site solar panels, to use later. It can keep the power on during an outage, for example, or meet the extra demand for electricity when everyone turns on their air-conditioning during a heat wave.

CHAPTER 10

IN IT FOR THE LONG HAUL

As Thanksgiving approached in 2017, a crowd gathered at SpaceX. Cameras flashed. iPhones were held high to capture what was coming . . . a truck. A freight-hauling, fully electric truck that looked as if it materialized from the future. The driver's seat sits in the middle of the cab. Its aerodynamic design actually had people cheering— about a truck. The semi came to a stop, and Elon stepped out to a rock star's welcome.

TAKE AWAY THE ARMOR: How does Elon come up with all these ideas and solutions to big problems? He lets ideas percolate, even if he's not actively working on something. He lets them simmer in the background, and as new clues and problem-solving pieces rise to the surface, he writes them down. Often, he says, the answers come while he's taking a shower.

Preaching to the crowd, Elon zipped through the Tesla Semi's stats. It could go zero to sixty in five seconds with just the cab and trailer. Fully loaded with eighty thousand pounds, the semi could still go from zero to sixty mph in twenty seconds. Other traditional truck models can't get anywhere near that. We've all seen it a million times. As your car tries to enter the highway, you get stuck behind a semi that's slowly accelerating to highway speed—it feels like slow motion. It takes a loooooong time. And not only was the Tesla truck powerful, it could also travel five hundred miles at highway speed on a single charge.

Production of the Tesla Semi is slated for 2019.

Tesla Semi. (Photo by Korbitr.)

After Elon wrapped up his presentation on the semi, he ordered the truck offstage and started to shake hands with people in the audience. The event seemed to be over. But then the sophisticated lighting design that gave the event such a big feel suddenly went dark. A red beam shone out from an oversized video screen. An animation began to play, and then you could see it. A view of the back of the semi's trailer. The door opened. The smoke of dry ice oozed out. Headlights lit up. And the semi's cargo was revealed to wild applause and cheering: a new, reimagined Roadster. This one, Elon said, would be available in 2020.

Elon's announcement made headlines around the world. At the same time, another story was brewing at Tesla: trouble producing the Model 3. The Model 3 had always been a big part of Tesla's business plan and was critical to Tesla's overall success as a company and its world-changing mission.

As cofounder Marc Tarpenning has explained: "Tesla had to come in at the high end. It was the only place with enough margin to play with. And that's why as Elon has pushed for the Model 3, that's the next big wave. 'Cause this is going to bring down the price to that of more like an Audi A4, which is going to enable hundreds and hundreds of thousands more people to be able to afford that—millions more people in the world. Ultimately we want to get electric cars everywhere. And it's going to be a tipping point. As they drive those prices down, as we understand the technology better, there is going to be a moment where everyone just goes, 'Oh, of course, I am going to drive an electric car."[136]

Tesla's Model Y. (© Tesla Motors Inc.)

In March 2019, Tesla added an electric compact SUV to its lineup, the Model Y. Along with seats for up to seven passengers, plenty of storage, and the safety features expected of SUVs, Elon promised something else—the feel and handling of a sports car. The mass-market vehicle is slated for delivery in 2020. The price will range from $39,000 to $60,000 depending on trim and options.

WHAT'S NEXT FOR TESLA? Elon asked Twitter followers what they'd like to see in a pickup truck. Design and engineering teams are already hard at work on a prototype.

Also announced with great fanfare early in November 2017, the Model 3's base price started at $35,000. Customers could reserve one with just $1,000. And it was said to be available immediately after preorders were delivered.

The goal? Produce twenty thousand Model 3s a month by December 2017. That date came and went, and only 260 Model 3s had been delivered. Elon assured the media that production would hit fifteen thousand cars a month by early 2018. But that date also came and went.

39A

MEANWHILE, THE ENGINEERS AT SPACEX HAD BEEN WORKING for years on a more powerful rocket, the Falcon Heavy. And in the winter of 2018, the world was watching Launchpad 39A. Part of the launch complex at Cape Canaveral, Florida, this was the spot where the Apollo astronauts blasted off on their way to the moon. This launchpad had sent space shuttles soaring.

But on February 6, 2018, it was SpaceX's Falcon Heavy that stood atop the historic launchpad. The most powerful rocket on the planet was ready for its first flight.

Falcon Heavy. (© SpaceX.)

FALCON HEAVY SPECS:

HEIGHT: 70 meters (229.6 feet)

WIDTH: 12.2 meters (39.9 feet)

ENGINES: 27 1st Stage Merlin engines

THRUST: Equal to eighteen 747 airplanes at full power

MASS: 1,420,788 kilograms (3,125,735 pounds)

The mission? A successful launch into orbit, release a test payload (usually a block of concrete), then land all three boosters back on Earth.

Crowds gathered at the nearby Kennedy Space Center. Cars and thousands of people lined the roads and highways, jockeying for a place to watch history. The media took up their positions to offer live coverage. Whether gathering near the launch site, watching on television, or streaming online—millions upon millions of people watched the countdown dwindle to the single digits.

LINGO ALERT! Max Q is the point in flight when the rocket is under maximum dynamic pressure from hurtling through the atmosphere. The mechanical stress on the structure's frame is at a peak, and it's a critical point in flight. What does Q have to do with it? Dynamic pressure is assigned the letter q in the formula to calculate it. When you watch a SpaceX launch, they are always marking the moment when a rocket reaches Max Q.

Humans were about to try do something otherworldly. And this enormous, years-long effort was *not* being led by a government agency, as all earlier space milestones had been. No, this effort was led by a *private* company. This effort was being led by a man with an even bigger vision of getting to Mars. This launch could be a huge accomplishment just by itself, but it also could be a huge leap toward a bigger space exploration dream.

Elon was in the control room, once again. And once again, everything was on the line. But with a much bigger audience. In fact, it was one of the most widely streamed live events in the history of YouTube.

National Geographic crews captured Elon's nerves. Hunched over, looking at the flight computers, he saw that all systems were green. In the final ten seconds, his eyes are focused, his mouth hanging open. Three. Two. One. He lifted his head to see what everyone else sees.

Falcon Heavy unleashed billowing clouds of dust, smoke, and flame as it raced toward space, shaking the ground below.

"That thing took off,"[137] he said, in near disbelief. He ran outside; everyone around him screamed or laughed out loud in utter amazement.

Falcon Heavy launch. (© SpaceX.)

Hand on his head, Elon smiled from ear to ear. The side boosters, fitted with cameras that were live streaming, had separated from the spacecraft and were making their way back to Earth.

Then they landed. *Simultaneously.*

The screaming from the crowd was off the charts. People cheered. People cried. Never had *anyone* seen anything like it.

Meanwhile, in orbit, the fairing or cargo bay was preparing to release the payload, but this wasn't a boring old block of concrete. *Instead* . . . when the fairing separated, the world met Starman, the spacesuit-clad mannequin driving Elon's very own shiny red Tesla Roadster. The radio was playing David Bowie's "Space Oddity" and, in large friendly letters on the dash, were the words DON'T PANIC, straight out of the pages of *The Hitchhiker's Guide to the Galaxy.* Elon had also sent Isaac Asimov's three Foundation books along for the ride— stored in the glove compartment on an optical disk made of quartz.

The phrase "Don't Panic," a nod to The Hitchhiker's Guide to the Galaxy *on the Roadster's dashboard. (© SpaceX.)*

Earthlings went crazy for the image. Starman had a *live* camera feed that broadcast a view of the mannequin driving the car, that blue marble behind him until he was too far out in the solar system to transmit the signal. The image made most front pages around the world the next day.

Starman and the Tesla Roadster in space. (© SpaceX.)

SEE FOR YOURSELF! SpaceX keeps the video of Starman on its YouTube channel.

Just as Elon originally intended to do with his green leaves on red Martian soil, that image captured the world's imagination. Space exploration was suddenly exciting again, and all along, Elon had been working on "the way." Imaginations captured, technology developing, everyday people began talking about when humans would get to Mars.

The U.S. Air Force awarded SpaceX a $130 million military contract for the Falcon Heavy to deliver a satellite into orbit. The mission is scheduled to launch in 2020. But, shhh! That's all we know. The mission is classified!

Dragon

Remember back in 2006 when SpaceX hadn't even had a successful launch yet? That's when NASA, due in large part to Gwynne Shotwell's efforts, awarded the company a contract to develop a spacecraft capable of delivering cargo to the International Space Station. And remember that $1.6 billion contract two days before Christmas in 2008? That was for twelve resupply flights to the space station. Those contracts allowed SpaceX to build Dragon, the cargo capsule, and Falcon 9, the rocket powerful enough to launch it into orbit.

On May 25, 2012, SpaceX made history when Dragon became the first commercial spacecraft to dock at the space station. "It looks like we've got us a Dragon by the tail,"[138] NASA astronaut Don Pettit said as the station's robotic arm reached out and grabbed the capsule.

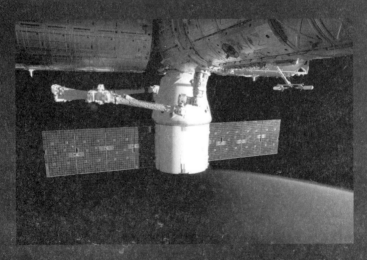

Dragon attached to the International Space Station. (© SpaceX.)

Astronauts are preparing to ride Crew Dragon in the future. SpaceX designed the capsule to carry people as well as cargo, and the first crew of astronauts is already in training. They must learn not only how to fly it, but how to handle any emergencies. Dragon's first crew will be NASA astronauts Victor Glover, Mike Hopkins, Bob Behnken, and Doug Hurley.

Dragon leaving SpaceX headquarters. (© SpaceX.)

This program became all the more critical in the fall of 2018 when a Russian Soyuz spacecraft experienced a rocket failure, 119 seconds after launch. Fortunately the emergency abort system kicked in and jettisoned the crew capsule away, and the astronaut and cosmonaut were unharmed. At the time, Russian spacecraft was the only way to get people to and from the space station. The pressure was on for SpaceX to get the Dragon crew ready and quick.

While astronauts undergo training in the module, its innovative escape system is also being tested. If Crew Dragon detects a problem with a booster, it could launch itself away from the booster and parachute back to Earth, then use reverse thrust to slowly land. So far, tests on the escape system have been successful.

Dragon splashdown. (© SpaceX.)

The first U.S. astronauts who will fly on American-made commercial spacecraft to and from the International Space Station, from left to right: Suni Williams, Josh Cassada, Eric Boe, Nicole Aunapu Mann, Chris Ferguson, Doug Hurley, Bob Behnken, Mike Hopkins, and Victor Glover. (© NASA.)

On March 2, 2019, Elon faced reporters, barely able to compose himself. Crew Dragon had just completed its successful demo launch and docked successfully with the International Space Station. Among the other cargo on board was "Ripley," the sensor-covered dummy dressed in a SpaceX space suit, named after the main character of the sci-fi movie *Alien*. The successful mission, Demo-1, not only paved the way for a launch with live astronauts on board, but also proved that NASA can rely on an American company to get to space—instead of the Russians.

MISSED DEADLINE: SpaceX didn't complete three demonstration launches for Dragon by 2009, but it still managed to send Dragon into orbit the next year. The spacecraft was required to carry actual cargo, so Elon placed a cheese wheel inside. It was a tribute to Monty Python.

MARS

or

BUST

I want to die on Mars.
Just not on impact.

—Elon Musk[139]

Imagine a colony on the Red Planet, people moving there and setting up the first Martian city. It will require engineers, medical crew, entrepreneurs, and scientists. To get started they'll need basic supplies, life-support systems, propellant, and a way to produce power. First, they'll build a base, then a city, and ultimately a civilization that sustains itself. That is Elon's dream, and he has a plan to achieve it.

Concept art of Starship *and Mars colony. (© SpaceX.)*

The plan calls for a new type of spaceship originally called the *Big Falcon Rocket*. It has since been renamed *Starship*. Construction of *Starship* is underway. The rocket will consist of a booster and a ship that can carry one to two hundred people on board.

But long before *Starship* attempts to take the first colonists to Mars, unmanned supply missions will drop off those critical necessities. The goal is to deliver cargo to Mars by 2022.

Starship will get a new name when the spaceship heads to Mars: *Heart of Gold*, which is the name of Elon's favorite spacecraft from *The Hitchhiker's Guide to the Galaxy*.

Concept art of sending Dragon *to Mars. (© SpaceX.)*

After launching the ship carrying the colonists into orbit, the *Starship*'s booster would quickly return to Earth, load up on fuel, and rejoin the colonists in space, resupplying the ship with enough fuel to make it to Mars. The trip would take about eighty days. SpaceX says the target date for crewed missions to Mars is 2024.

Elon's bigger vision is that SpaceX will take a million people to Mars over a hundred year period. But the plan is constantly evolving as technology evolves.

"I think we are working on one of the most important things we possibly can, and that's to find another place for humans to live and survive and thrive. If something happened on Earth, you need humans living somewhere else,"[140] SpaceX president Gwynne Shotwell said.

ROUND-TRIP ROCKET TICKETS

BECAUSE A HUMAN CIVILIZATION ON MARS IS AN IDEA WITH a huge price tag, you need a way to pay for it. Elon's solution: Develop a spacecraft that can not only ferry people back and forth to Mars, but carry out a number of other jobs, like launching satellites for governments and businesses and providing transportation from Earth to the moon.

Starship would more than double the power of the Falcon Heavy, which dramatically increases the type of payloads the spacecraft can carry and where those payloads can be delivered. It could place much larger satellites and telescopes into space, giving scientists the opportunity to "see really incredible things and discover incredible things in space,"[141] Gwynne explained in a recent TED Talk. All of those missions would bring in revenue.

But this rocket could also take you to the other side of *this* planet—in just forty-five minutes. True space-age travel on a spaceship that can take you from one point on Earth to another. And the best part is, the longest part of the trip will be the boat ride to and from the landing pads.

"It's definitely going to happen,"[142] Gwynne said during her onstage interview.

"If I can do this trip in half an hour to an hour, I can do dozens of these a day, right?" Gwynne explained. "And yet, a long-haul aircraft can only make one of those flights a day. So even if my rocket was slightly more expensive and the fuel is a little bit more expensive, I can run ten times, at least, what they are running a day and really make the revenue I need to out of that system."[143]

When could rocketing to Asia become a real thing? Well, according to Gwynne, by 2028.

Colonial Internet

Okay, so there are plans in place for getting to and for colonizing the Red Planet. Um, but what about when they get there? You are going to want the Internet available to keep in touch with Earth while chilling (or engaging in your daily fight for survival) on Mars. In January 2015, Elon announced his plans to develop a space-based Internet called Starlink.

The first step is providing satellite-based Internet for all of Earth. The satellites, some four *thousand* of them, would beam down broadband Internet from low Earth orbit. The price tag for a space-based Internet? $10 billion. And the number of people on the planet who would have improved access or their first access at all to the Internet? Roughly three billion.

"Yeah, there is no question," SpaceX president Gwynne Shotwell said. "It will change the world."[144]

It took a while, but in 2018 Elon finally won approval from the Federal Communications Commission for his plan to build a global broadband network using SpaceX satellites. Elon has approval to launch a whopping 4,425 satellites to create his Starlink network.

When Elon first announced the project, he made his ultimate goal clear. Eventually he wanted his network to deliver an Internet to Mars. "It will be important for Mars to have a global communications network as well," he said, adding, "I don't see anyone else doing it."[145]

THIS IS THE BORING BIT

In the spring of 2018, Gary took center stage for a big talk. Only, Gary is a snail, so he let his speed do the talking. Like all snails, he is slow. Sluggish. Even so, Gary has a target on his back because he's been winning a race against Elon Musk. Like Elon, Gary lives in Los Angeles—which is full of Hollywood stars, people who want to become Hollywood stars, palm trees, surfers, talent agents, writers, and... traffic. Epic traffic. Go-one-mile-in-one-hour traffic.

On this topic, Elon never minces words. "So right now, I think one of the most soul-destroying things is traffic," he said during a TED Talk. "It affects people in every part of the world. It takes away so much of your life. It's horrible. It's particularly horrible in L.A."[146] Soul. Destroying.

Elon's goal is to solve the traffic problem by *boring* tunnels under big cities. Then after the tunnels are dug, you need something to zip through them. Something that doesn't create another traffic disaster, even a subterranean one. His solution harks back to that high-speed travel idea Elon had years ago—a system of vacuum tunnels to transport people and vehicles. But for it to work, tunnel digging and building must speed up—by a factor of ten!

What's this got to do with Gary? The snail hangs out at the Boring Company, a subsidiary of SpaceX founded to bore tunnels for high-speed travel.

Gary is the company pet, kind of a mascot really—and also a goal.

What's the spark of inspiration for Gary's name? Gary, the snail from *SpongeBob SquarePants*. The Boring Company's Gary even lives in a pineapple-shaped terrarium.

Gary the snail. (© The Boring Company.)

"Gary is capable of going fourteen times faster than a tunnel-boring machine," Elon admitted, explaining the score. "We want to beat Gary ... Victory will be beating the snail."[147]

SNAIL SPEED: The average garden snail is capable of speeds of 0.029 mph. Sloths? The three-toed sloth tops out at 0.15 mph. Walking humans usually hit between 2 to 3 mph (faster if they are late for class!).

It's funny—for now. But when their tunnel-boring machine catches up to Gary or steals Gary's slimy snail-trail lead, that's when some really exciting things could happen to send "soul-destroying" traffic to the history books.

"The fundamental issue that we face is that so much of our life is 3-D. You're in a tall building or in a dense office environment and then we go to this 2-D plane of streets. And the consequences are obvious," Elon said at a company information session. "You're like losing an entire dimension."[148]

In other words, you go from many floors of office space, down to a lobby and out to a single layer street. And you do this at predictable times along with all the other people who work there: at 9:00 a.m., lunchtime, and quittin' time.

"So then obviously you are going to get stuck in traffic. Guaranteed. But if you can do hundreds of tunnels and you can have many small stations woven throughout the fabric of the city, without even the city appearing any different, you could solve the transport problem."[149]

The high-speed transportation system is called Loop.

LOOP:

SPEED: 125–150 mph

EMISSIONS: Zero (electric power)

BORING PREDICTION: Downtown Los Angeles to LAX airport would take eight minutes.

"It's almost like an autonomous underground multilevel car system,"[150] Elon explained. The Loop would have its own mass transit cars, or Autonomous Electric Vehicles (AEV), some of which would be built on extended Model X chassis. But other AEVs would travel through the tunnel system using guide wheels that would deploy from your car when you enter the Loop. Once deployed, your car would function more like a train as it moves through the tunnels. When you exit, the guide wheels would retract back under your car. Or, other iterations have included electric "skates" that move cars through the system. The Boring Company is continuing research and development on how to best move people, and their vehicles, through the system. The idea is to have unlimited tunnels to unlimited places so that you can take high-speed mass transit directly to your destination without making a billion unnecessary stops, the way you do on modern subway systems.

"There's no real limit to how many levels of tunnels you can have. You can go much further deep than you can go up," Elon said. "The deepest mines are much deeper than the tallest buildings are tall, so you can alleviate any arbitrary level of urban congestion with a 3-D tunnel network. This is a very important point."[151]

Bottom line? This idea isn't about digging a single tunnel to fix traffic on the roads. It's about digging as many tunnels as required in

Concept art for a Boring Company pod. (© The Boring Company.)

the ground as deep as they need to be dug, one on top of another on top of another—until traveling and commuting is not that big a deal. They are even experimenting with the idea of an elevator that takes you from your garage to the tunnel system!

"We are trying to maximize the usefulness of the system while having it not affect people's lives as it gets created,"[152] Elon said. Not affecting people's lives—that means no noise, no vibrations, no effect on quality of life. According to the Boring Company, you will not see them, feel them, or hear them. Generally, not making people mad.

And as for the "usefulness" part of that statement, that means potentially tying in to existing mass transportation.

Elon said this idea also gets rid of two other big problems: (1) slicing and dicing communities with big highways and (2) large subway stations that take up so much room and have to accommodate a lot of people coming and going. Elon's proposal is for tons of small stations, no bigger than a couple of parking spaces. But to pull this off, they still have to wrestle with the speed of tunnel boring and bringing new technology, new ways of thinking to the process.

Typically, when tunnels are built, construction crews must drill, then stop, then remove dirt, then put in structural reinforcements. But the Boring Company's plan centers on continuous drilling and placing reinforcement segments at the same time. And instead of laying heavy and expensive electrical cable in miles of tunnel to power the boring machine, the company's machine will use Tesla battery packs. On top of that, the project has been getting support from top engineering talent from both Tesla and SpaceX.

The Boring Machine. (© The Boring Company.)

While attempting to solve the traffic problem through the Boring Company's tunnel-transport quest, Elon has stumbled on to a couple of other solutions . . . for entirely different problems.

YOUR BACKYARD PYRAMID

FORTY-TWO IS THE ANSWER. BUT WHAT IS THE QUESTION? That's part of the story in *The Hitchhiker's Guide to the Galaxy*. Similarly, in solving one problem Elon sometimes stumbles on a random answer. And then he looks for the question. It happened at the Boring Company, and the answer was dirt. Lots and lots of dirt. That's what happens when you dig holes, right? You end up with lots of dirt. But if dirt was the answer, what was the question? Just like a *Jeopardy!* contestant, Elon came up with the question: What is a cheap ingredient to make really strong bricks?

Well, his company began mixing the dirt with a small amount of concrete. Then it compressed the mixture using a lot of pressure . . . which made really strong bricks. In fact, the company says the bricks meet California's stringent earthquake code. It is possible that the Boring Company will offer them for sale for construction. Elon said he's even tossing around the idea of making life-sized Lego kits with the bricks that you could buy and construct in your backyard! "It seems like a fun way to spend an afternoon,"[153] he said.

As of this writing, the Lego-like kits are not for sale, but Elon set the price at ten cents a brick, well below what other bricks and concrete blocks cost. And while using the bricks for backyard Legos sounds super fun, he was quick to point out that the bricks could potentially be used to build affordable housing as well. And on that point, there was no doubt that he was serious.

Elon Musk stands behind a podium made of the Boring Company's bricks.
(Photo by Robyn Beck/AFP/Getty Images.)

So calling the company boring is kind of funny because it really is anything but. From creating subterranean high-speed travel to creating life-sized buildable bricks to Elon's tweet that the Boring Company would sell . . . um . . . flamethrowers, which he renamed Not a Flamethrower to get around shipping regulations. And if we are getting technical, Elon said in an interview, "It's actually just a roofing torch with an air rifle cover. It's not a real flamethrower."[154]

The idea for the flamethrower came from one of Elon's favorite movies, a hilarious spoof of *Star Wars* called *Spaceballs*. The sci-fi parody hit theaters in 1987 and developed a cult following.

In *Spaceballs*, Yogurt (not the food, but the Yoda-like character brought to life by actor Mel Brooks, who also wrote and directed the movie) is explaining the concept of merchandising to the movie's stars. "What is it?" they ask. And Yogurt opens the door to a hidden store of mementos and trinkets with the movie's title printed on each and every item.

"Merchandising! Merchandising!" Yogurt barks. "Where the real money from the movie is made. *Spaceballs* the T-shirt! *Spaceballs* the coloring book! *Spaceballs* the lunch box! *Spaceballs* the breakfast cereal!" Yogurt holds up something kind of awkward and announces, "*Spaceballs* the flamethrower. The kids love this one!"[155]

That was it. Elon knew what kind of merchandise he wanted: a flamethrower. The Boring Company needed to raise $10 million, and as Elon said, "that was twenty thousand flamethrowers at five hundred dollars each."[156] They sold out in four days.

The media, Twittersphere, and other corners of the Internet wondered if it was a joke. But in June 2018, Elon hosted a Not a Flamethower pickup party. Happy customers arrived to pick up their merch and quickly tweeted pictures of themselves giving the giant torch a test run.

Elon's Twitter thread about the Boring Company's Not a Flamethrower (screenshot taken October 2018).

DIG IN

IN THE SUMMER OF 2018, ELON AND MAYOR RAHM EMANUEL stood before the Chicago press corps to make an announcement. The Boring Company had won the bid to build an Express Loop from downtown Chicago to O'Hare International Airport.

> The Express Loop, called the X, will be entirely funded by the Boring Company and its investors.

Driving to the airport in a car during rush hour currently takes at least an hour. In the proposed Express Loop, with pods traveling thirty to sixty feet underground at an estimated 125 mph, it will take just twelve minutes. And while a traditional taxi ride sets travelers back around $50, the Express Loop is estimated to cost about half that. Each pod can carry more than a dozen travelers. The entire fleet of battery-powered pods could transport up to two thousand passengers an hour, with pods departing every thirty seconds to two minutes.

"Chicago is giving us the opportunity to show that [the Loop] can be useful and economically viable on a large scale," Elon said. "One of the hardest things to do with any new technology is not to demonstrate that technology and show that it works but to show people that it can be indeed useful. It's one of the hardest things in the world—to make something useful."[157]

The announcement was met with a ton of questions, mostly about safety. At the time of the announcement, the project was still early in its development. Elon said a lot of questions would be answered as more details are refined.

Digging is also underway in Los Angeles for a high-speed tunnel to Dodger Stadium.

When asked what they would say to doubters, Mayor Emanuel responded, "It's easy to be a critic or a cynic. What jobs do they produce? What economic growth do they produce? When Chicago decided to be the first city to take the intercontinental railroad system, it surpassed St. Louis within twenty years. When Chicago decided to be a leader in aviation, you saw what happened to its economy. Were there doubters about O'Hare? Were there doubters about the intercontinental? Yes. There are doubters along the way all the time who sit on the sidelines. And then when the thing gets built and the opportunities come and the job growth happens, you can't find them."[158]

Will Elon be responsible for reinventing how people travel from place to place? Every time that question comes up, Elon points to SpaceX. In 2002, zero people believed he could pull off forming a private space exploration company. Zero. Today, he's reinvented how rockets are made and flown.

BOOKSHELF! *Structures: Or Why Things Don't Fall Down* by J. E. Gordon. Elon's take? He says the book is fantastic for understanding the basics of structural design.

EXTRA LOOPY

THERE'S LOOP AND THEN THERE'S *HYPER*LOOP. THERE'S HIGH speed and then there's something just shy of teleportation. Imagine entering a pressurized pod in a vacuum tube that can take you from San Francisco to Los Angeles in roughly thirty minutes. As we have already talked about, Elon was no stranger to the epic Bay Area–LA commute. And all of those trips back and forth sparked daydreams about this new sci-fi level of transportation.

All the way back in 2013 he mused about the whole thing while visiting the team behind the online learning nonprofit Khan Academy. In an interview with Sal Khan, Elon said, "I was reading about the California high-speed rail, and it was quite depressing. Because California taxpayers are going to be on the hook to build the most expensive high-speed rail per mile in the world—and the slowest," he said. "Those are not the superlatives you want."[159]

So he began doing what Elon does: breaking down transportation to its fundamental purpose and parts. And then he started rearranging those ingredients.

"If you just say, 'What would you ideally want in a transportation system?' You'd say, okay, well, you'd want something that relative to existing modes of transportation is faster. Let's say twice as fast, costs half as much per ticket, can't crash, is immune to weather, and you can make the whole thing self-powering with solar panels."[160]

What could do that? His answer was a vacuum tunnel with pods that travel around 300 mph.

Why a vacuum? Because it eliminates air friction, enabling the pod to travel at much greater speeds.

Five years later, he's built a Hyperloop vacuum tube for testing that's 0.8 miles long and six feet in diameter. It sits right outside SpaceX headquarters and tests pods traveling at speeds of 200 mph (braking just in time). The video of a test run moves so fast that before Elon played it at an information session, he gave the audience a seizure warning.

The goal is to get the test pod up to speeds over 300 mph, comparable to jets. Only a pod in a vacuum won't have the same physical limitations of a jet. "We don't really have mach problems. We aren't creating massive sonic booms because we evacuated the air,"[161] Elon said. "We built a Hyperloop test track adjacent to SpaceX, just for a student competition, to encourage innovative ideas in transport. And it actually ends up being the biggest vacuum chamber in the world after the Large Hadron Collider, by volume."[162]

Students are designing potential pods? Yes. That first year, 2015, over a thousand universities worldwide entered the competition. The proposals were narrowed down to twenty, and the students tested their designs at SpaceX. The fastest pod that can stop without crashing wins. In 2017, the winning pod clocked 201 mph!

In December 2018, the Boring Company unveiled a 1.1 mile-long test tunnel. Plans for other tunnels are underway. But this sneak peek featured a Tesla with retractable side wheels that allowed a Model X to drive autonomously directly on the concrete tracks. This demo was more of a proof of concept to give people an idea of what this project will look and feel like when it comes to life. There is still more work to be done and problems to be solved. But the test tunnels will allow for tons of research on both the Loop and the Hyperloop.

The Hawthorne test tunnel as of October 28, 2017. (© The Boring Company.)

EARTHQUAKE! What would happen in the tunnel during an earthquake? Experts say one of the safest places to be during an earthquake is in a tunnel. Seismic motion becomes greater as it approaches the surface, and most tunnels are reinforced and built to withstand seismic activity.

And as with Loop development, not only are Boring Company employees working on the Hyperloop project, but so are some of the top engineers from SpaceX.

"We are taking world-class engineering talent, applying it to this problem, and seeing if we can make some headway,"[163] Elon said.

Ad Astra

This Latin phrase means "to the stars." But it is also the name of a private school that Elon started to educate his five boys. Today, the school is located inside SpaceX and has forty students.

There are no grades like first, second, third. It's a project-based curriculum that strives to make education hands-on and take advantage of kids' curiosity, while getting them comfortable with problem-solving. Students grapple with real-world subjects like robotics and artificial intelligence. All in the middle of a rocket factory. This is an outside-the-box school.

This concept is a far cry from what Elon experienced when he was a schoolboy. While Elon easily annihilated math, even math beyond his grade level, he struggled with other subjects like South Africa's Afrikaans language. But his performance had to do more with philosophy than ability. "I just didn't see the point of learning that. It seemed ridiculous. I'd get a passing grade and that was fine," Elon told biographer Ashlee Vance. "I'd rather play video games, write software, and read books than try and get an A if there's no point in getting an A."[164]

Ad Astra may be focused on teaching technology, math, critical thinking, etc., but that said, *Ars Technica* published a scoop on the school, revealing there is, in fact, time every day for dodgeball.

CHAPTER 13

DANGER

"Climate change is the biggest threat that humanity faces this century, except for AI," Elon said in his interview with *Rolling Stone*. "I keep telling people this. I hate to be the Cassandra here, but it's all fun and games until somebody loses [an] eye."[165]

Artificial intelligence is an emerging technology. So the precise definition will change as its development and use is better understood. But loosely, when people talk about *general* artificial intelligence today, they are talking about computers that can think, reason, and learn like humans. Limited or task-specific AI uses computers for tasks that would normally require human beings, such as analyzing medical X-rays or translating languages between speakers or even flipping hamburgers.

During the spring of 2018, Elon took to Twitter to convince people to watch a new documentary about artificial intelligence, *Do You Trust This Computer?* It was produced by Chris Paine. This wasn't Chris's first documentary. In 2006, the filmmaker produced a documentary about GM's EV1 debacle. (Remember the car that was leased to owners, then taken back and crushed? The funeral held by sad drivers? The candlelight vigils?) He then followed it up with *Revenge of the Electric Car*, which included part of Tesla's story.

In this new documentary about artificial intelligence, Elon outlined his concerns. "We are rapidly headed towards digital superintelligence that far exceeds any human, and I think it's very obvious,"[166] he said. And to Elon, the threat to humans is obvious too.

"AI doesn't have to be evil to destroy humanity," Elon further explained. "If AI has a goal and humanity just happens to be in the way, it will destroy humanity as a matter of course, without even thinking about it. No hard feelings. It's just like if we are building a road and an anthill happens to be in the way, we don't hate ants. We are just building a road. And so, good-bye anthill."[167]

Elon is not the only one who has expressed concerns of this kind. One of the world's greatest minds, the late Stephen Hawking, laid it out in plain language. In an interview with the BBC in 2014, the theoretical physicist said, "The development of full artificial intelligence could spell the end of the human race."[168]

There is no question that AI will soon touch almost everything humans do. Artificial intelligence is already present in cell phones and e-mail functions like predictive text and navigation. Google Translate underwent mind-blowing overnight improvements when it switched to machine learning instead of humans sitting there programming the service with grammar rules, vocabulary, etc. Examples are endless and growing. Google Assistant announced an AI-based feature that will make actual real-life phone calls on your behalf to schedule things like hair appointments and restaurant reservations. In a 2018 demo, when the computer called a hair salon, the receptionist who picked up didn't even realize a computer was calling—that's how good the computer was at sounding human.

So there are seriously helpful applications for AI. It can even be used to sift through massive amounts of scientific data and make important discoveries (such as previously unknown exoplanets in the galaxy). And that's before you get to medical applications of the lifesaving variety, like cancer detection.

But this technology also comes with ethical and moral dilemmas, including, Will this technology kill us?

Part of the problem, as Elon sees it, is that we don't generally think things through. We invent. We discover problems with our invention, and then we try to fix them—which usually takes years. Cars are a great example. At first they didn't have seat belts. In crashes, people died regularly. Having not thought through how to keep bodies safe in a crash, car companies had to figure it out later and came up with seat belts. But it took years for a law to actually make seat belts mandatory and set a universal safety standard.

Elon's point is, Why not think it all the way through first? Why not start with regulations and ethics and a clear idea of what the problems could be—so we can avoid them.

Elon even took his concerns directly to President Barack Obama and to a meeting of all fifty governors. "I met with Obama for one reason"—to talk about the dangers of artificial intelligence.[169]

In 2015, Elon cofounded a nonprofit called OpenAI to research the development of AI and how can AI be used to benefit humanity instead of . . . um . . . to annihilate us.

> OpenAI is a nonprofit "AI research company, discovering and enacting the path to safe artificial general intelligence."[170]

"It's going to be very tempting to use AI as a weapon. In fact, it will be used as a weapon. The on-ramp to serious AI, the danger is going to be more humans using it against each other, I think, most likely. That will be the danger,"[171] he explained in a podcast with Joe Rogan.

As of this writing, OpenAI has a team of sixty researchers and engineers working on the project, and they conduct their research without the pressure of having to make money. Sponsors include Elon, Peter Thiel, Microsoft, Infosys, and Amazon.

In 2018, to avoid a conflict of interest, Elon resigned from the board because Tesla is using AI in its development of self-driving technology. That being said, Elon remains an adviser.

"I think it's incredibly important that AI not be 'other.' It must be us," Elon explained. "But I think we are really going to have to merge with AI or be left behind."[172]

And in fact, Elon has another company called Neuralink that's attempting to do just that.

BOOKSHELF! *Our Final Invention: Artificial Intelligence and the End of the Human Era* by James Barrat

CYBORG

FORGET HYBRID CARS. WHAT IF YOU COULD HAVE A HYBRID brain? Part natural brain with a huge assist from a tiny supercomputer. Access to the world's knowledge? The capacity to communicate without speaking? Or typing?

"We have a bandwidth problem," Elon said. "You just can't communicate through your fingers. They are just too slow."[173]

There is still not a lot known about the scope of Neuralink's work. The company's simple website says, "Neuralink is developing ultrahigh bandwidth brain-machine interfaces to connect humans and computers."[174]

It's a type of brain-computer interface that could give you superhuman intelligence. It's possible the interface may involve what's called neural lace, an ultrathin mesh of electrodes implanted directly in your skull.

Elon believes that people already have "some sort of merger with biological intelligence and machine intelligence. To some degree we are already a cyborg, if you think of the digital tools you have—your phone, your computer, the applications,"[175] he said in 2017 at the World Government Summit in Dubai.

"Over time I think we'll probably see a closer merger of biological intelligence and digital intelligence, and it's mostly about the bandwidth, the speed of the connection between your brain and the digital extension of yourself."

As Elon sees it, the bottleneck is output. Our poor thumbs can't keep up with expressing what's happening in our brains. "So some high bandwidth interface to the brain, I think, will be something that helps achieve a symbiosis between human and machine intelligence,"[176] Elon said. In other words, if our typing thumbs, fingers, and verbal communication is holding back our output, what would we be able to communicate or investigate if a computer in our brains could open the floodgates?

There are huge questions about the whole idea. Is it possible? Is it ethical? Is it a matter of survival? All of those remain to be seen. Stay tuned.

XPRIZE

Ad Astra isn't Elon's only interest in education. Elon provided $15 million for the Global Learning XPRIZE, dedicated to solving one of education's biggest challenges. The idea is for children in developing countries to teach themselves basic reading, writing, and math—with the support of technology. Four thousand children in Tanzania received tablet computers to test five teams' teaching software over fifteen months. The five finalists were selected from 198 teams around the world and given $1 million each to develop their technology. The team that achieves the best results with the students will win a grand prize of $10 million.

PRODUCTION HELL

Technology "does *not* automatically improve. It only improves if a lot of people work very hard to make it better. And actually, it will, I think, by itself, degrade," Elon explained in his 2017 TED Talk. "You look at great civilizations like ancient Egypt, and they were able to make the pyramids, and they forgot how to do that. And the Romans, they built these incredible aqueducts. They forgot how to do it."[177]

Elon doesn't know how long we have to save humanity. And he thinks of it like that. The window is open now, but no one knows for how long.

That urgency is what drives him to take on more and more

problems and hunt down solutions. He's working against the clock, and that pressure is ever present for him.

The Falcon Heavy's debut may have dazzled earthlings, but meanwhile—back at the Tesla factory—a different story was brewing. Elon summed it up in two telling words: production hell.

The problem child was the Model 3. It was designed and hailed as the car for the masses. Now in production, the demand and buzz was white hot. Customers couldn't wait to get their hands on it. The media couldn't wait. Investors couldn't wait. And yet there was delay after delay. Problem after problem. Tesla was not producing them quickly enough. Elon had to figure it out. And fast.

Sure, Elon was by now a billionaire, with multiple houses in Bel-Air, but for the foreseeable future, he wasn't resting his head on a cushy pillow at home, surrounded by all the creature comforts that come with that kind of money. No, he moved into the factory to work there and *sleep* there. During his waking hours, Elon could be found on the factory floor, helping teams work through problems and bottlenecks. When it was time to sleep, Elon claimed a spot on a couch in a conference room. If there was a problem in the middle of the night, he wanted his team to wake him up so he could help solve it.

The media seized on the story. Was Tesla going bankrupt? Would it survive? Was the CEO out of control, out of touch, over the edge? These were the conversations on national and international television. Newspapers, blogs, and podcasts joined in. It was constant chatter about Tesla and Elon.

Then, in the middle of production hell, Elon attended the social function of the year: the Met Gala. It is the see-and-be-seen event to beat all others. Picture Hollywood's biggest movie stars, the wealthiest tech moguls, beautiful supermodels, all coming together in elaborate evening wear chosen to fit a specific theme. For heaven's sake, it was put on by *Vogue*'s iconic editor Anna Wintour, and another organizer was Amal Clooney, the famous human rights attorney who happens to be married to actor George Clooney.

As he climbed the steps of the Metropolitan Museum of Art in New York City, and walked past the hordes of media waiting to catch a glimpse of every celebrity, he was not alone. Elon had a date, his new girlfriend, synth-pop artist Grimes. Their very public debut was putting the world on notice. He'd found love again.

Elon Musk and Claire Elise Boucher, aka Grimes, at the Met Gala.
(Photo by Anthony Behar/Sipa USA via AP Images.)

Grimes, aka Claire Elise Boucher, is a musician. In 2018, she recorded the theme song for popular graphic-novel-turned-animated TV show *Hilda*, and Apple featured Grimes and her creative process during a big computing ad campaign. She met Elon over Twitter when she made a joke about AI. As Elon went to make the same joke, he realized Grimes had beat him to the punch.

Their appearance sent entertainment reporters, Twitter, and a hefty percentage of Elon's and Grimes's fans into gossipfest overdrive! It was *the* talk. But after their big night out, Elon was back on the plane, and back at the factory, focused on the problem at hand: scaling Model 3 production.

When CBS's Gayle King toured the production line in the spring of 2018, Elon told her, "I'm definitely under stress, so if I seem like I'm not under stress then I'm gonna be clear, I'm definitely under stress."[178]

The goal had been to produce five thousand cars a week. By April 2018, the number was less than half that. That was a problem because manufacturing and selling a massive amount of Model 3s *was and still is* the fundamental point of having a mass-market car. It was also critical to Tesla's business plan.

Elon began personally tackling every problem, including the admitted use of too many robots in assembly. While Elon was dealing with Model 3 production, Tesla issued a recall of 123,000 Model S cars. That meant more headlines.

The voluntary recall was for an issue with the power steering. The problem was caused by road salt used in colder regions to melt ice and snow on the road. It could corrode or beak down power steering bolts. When that happened, it made it harder to steer the car at low speeds. The solution was to replace the bolts.

Moody's, a leading financial analyst and research company on Wall Street, downgraded Tesla's credit rating, pointing to the Model 3 production shortfall. That meant even more headlines.

Then, that spring a driver was killed in a horrible car accident while driving his Tesla Model X. The media called into question the safety of Tesla's semiautonomous autopilot. A few months later, an investigation by the National Transportation Safety Board offered a preliminary clue as to what happened, saying the driver did not have his hands on the wheel for six seconds immediately before it crashed.

May 8, 2018, brought another deadly accident, which meant another investigation. Speeding at 116 mph around a 25 mph curve, the eighteen-year-old driver lost control of his Model S and crashed. Not only was the driver killed, but one of his passengers died too. Another passenger was injured.

When emergency crews got to the scene of the crash, one aspect of the wreckage stood out: the battery fire. Investigators said it took three hundred gallons of foam and water to extinguish the flames. Adding to that, the Model S's batteries reignited twice, once on the tow truck and again after the wrecked car was placed in a storage yard. As of this writing, that issue is still under investigation. Part of what they are looking into is how first responders worked to extinguish the flames. Could first responders be in danger at the scene of a crash involving a Tesla Model S? Meanwhile, since speed was a factor in the crash, Tesla added a speed limiter feature to its software in honor of the teen who was killed.

TESLA WORKPLACE SAFETY. Is Tesla a safe place to work? In 2017, investigative reporters at the *Guardian* published a report looking into worker injuries. The article cited hundreds of ambulance calls to the factory since 2014. The article featured interviews with fifteen factory workers, including former workers. One worker, Richard Ortiz, was quoted as saying, "Everything feels like the future but us."[179]

In response to the allegations, Elon explained how much he cared about his workers and that the safety record was improving. The article also featured interviews with workers who were happy about their job, workplace conditions, and benefits. In April 2018, California's Division of Occupational Safety and Health opened an investigation into whether Tesla was underreporting workplace injuries. These investigations typically take at least several months to complete.

A chorus of critics seemed to speak in unison. Could Tesla's failure be close at hand? Were Tesla's automobiles dangerous? The tension spilled over into Elon's direct interactions with the media and even on earnings conference calls with financial analysts and investors. He was angry about what he called "bone-headed, boring" questions. He was furious about the media's lack of context in reporting on Tesla. He specifically pointed out that when Tesla was involved in an accident, it made national headlines. The same standard is not applied to every other carmaker and the thousands of car crashes that happen daily.

A prime example? Also in May 2018, a Model S hit a stopped truck at 60 mph and was left nearly unrecognizable. The accident had two competing storylines. Media headlines ran with the driver's account that the autopilot was on at the time. Elon, in complete exasperation, pointed out that other than a broken foot, the driver was fine. For Elon, this was testament to the car's safety.

He weighed in on Twitter: "What's actually amazing about this accident is that a Model S hit a fire truck at 60mph and the driver only broke an ankle. An impact at that speed usually results in severe injury or death."[180]

The tension between Elon and his critics and the media filled into Elon's Twitter feed. That snowballed into more bad coverage. Headlines read: ELON MUSK'S MEDIA MELTDOWN; ELON MUSK LASHES OUT AT MEDIA, AGAIN; ELON MUSK'S SILLY WAR WITH THE MEDIA; and more.

While tweeting, Elon proposed a solution: Pravduh, an online rating of journalists' credibility. The media seemed unprepared for such a direct and public attack on their coverage. Eventually the full display of a nasty back and forth simmered down. It's yet to be seen if Elon will follow through with rolling out Pravduh.

Elon Musk's tweets about Pravduh (screenshot taken October 2018).

At the same time a *Consumer Reports* review of the Model 3 nailed the car for poor brake performance. As a result, the car did not receive the magazine's coveted recommendation. Tesla immediately tweaked the brakes with an over-the-air fix. Then, *Consumer Reports* experts retested the car and the results allowed the magazine to give the Model 3 the gold standard "buy" recommendation. Tough headlines ultimately gave way to *Consumer Reports'* awed acknowledgment that Tesla fixed the problem in *one week*, using a software update. Tesla did not have to haul cars back to the factory or a service center. Engineers simply reprogrammed the braking system and sent the fix wirelessly to the cars. It was a stunning development.

At the factory, Elon added an additional assembly line . . . in the parking lot, under a tent. It flew in the face of standard auto assembly, where cars are supposed to be made in giant factory buildings, but as a solution, it was a classic start-up maneuver—nimble, innovative, new thinking that thumbed its nose at convention. And Elon was thrilled, snapping pictures and tweeting them to the world.

Tesla assembly line. (© Tesla Motors Inc.)

And it worked. By the end of the third quarter of 2018, Tesla was making five thousand Model 3s a week.

As he thanked Tesla owners and workers, the media moved the goal. Could Tesla do it the next week and the next? Was its success a fluke? Would Tesla turn a profit? Or would it still go bankrupt?

The pressure remained and intensified. And Elon erupted.

In a single tweet one August morning, Elon said, "Am considering taking Tesla private at $420. Funding secured."[181] The tweet hit in the middle of the trading day in New York and sent Tesla's stock price soaring by 6 percent. The Securities and Exchange Commission decided to take a look because such a statement from a CEO who is also the chairman of the board could affect the company's stock price.

Elon Musk's August 7 tweets (screenshot taken October 30, 2018).

This was the big question: Did Elon really have funding secured? The public backlash was swift and immediate. Elon backed down from taking the company private. In September the SEC charged Elon with securities fraud in federal court, saying his tweet was false and misleading. Ultimately, Elon and Tesla settled. Tesla was fined

$20 million. Elon was personally fined $20 million, and while he would remain CEO, he would no longer be chairman of the board.

> Tesla has more than forty thousand employees. As of November 2018, the company was valued at $56 billion.

Elon was not happy. Shortly after the settlement was announced, Elon mockingly renamed the SEC the Shortseller Enrichment Commission. When asked about the fine on Twitter, he replied, "Worth it."

But then he threw the biggest punch he had and the one he loves most—success. Model 3 safety test results were in, and they were stellar. The car received the coveted five-star safety rating, and that's not all. It also had the lowest probability of injury, which makes the Model 3 one of the safest cars ever tested by the National Highway Traffic Safety Administration.

There was another reason to crow . . . the company had made a profit of $312 million and was expected to be profitable going forward.

And that led to headlines like this. *Forbes:* GUESS WHAT? EVERYONE WAS WRONG ABOUT TESLA. CNN: MEET THE NEW, PROFITABLE TESLA. *USA Today*: TESLA DELIVERS PROFIT.

> **SPOTLIGHT:** Meet the chair of the Tesla board: Robyn M. Denholm. Robyn had been part of Tesla's board since August 2014. She was also COO of a telecommunications company called Telstra. When her appointment was announced, Robyn mentioned how much she loves Tesla's mission and looks forward to helping Elon and the team reach their goals.

Controversy or not, bad press or good press—there is a huge stick by which Elon is measuring Tesla, his core mission: Is this company helping to save the planet? He took on a car industry that was turning its back on electric cars, and now he had them twisted up in knots trying to get electric vehicles on the market as soon as possible.

"The fundamental value of a company like Tesla is the degree to which it accelerates the advent of sustainable energy, faster than it would otherwise occur," Elon explained during his TED Talk. "So when I think like, What is the fundamental good of Tesla? I would say, hopefully, if it accelerated that by a decade, or potentially more than a decade, that would be quite a good thing."[182]

> Will he remain CEO? Elon's goal with Tesla from the beginning was for Tesla to jump-start the world's interest in electric cars, production of electric cars, and use of electric cars. Success for Elon is when a gas-guzzling car is an exception on the road and on the sales floor. That's a very different goal. And he has said that when there are more electric cars than not, that's when he'll step down as CEO.

> **BOOKSHELF!** Elon's thoughts on oil were partly shaped by *Merchants of Doubt: How a Handful of Scientists Obscured the Truth on Issues from Tobacco Smoke to Global Warming* by Naomi Oreskes and Erik M. Conway.

The Future

In the immediate future Elon sees a reality where your car drops you off at work, and while you sit at your cubicle, the car heads off to pick up your laundry. Or the car heads off to pick up other people you've shared it with. Then the car is back in time to pick you up when you are ready.

"There will be a shared autonomy fleet where you buy your car, and you can choose to use that car exclusively. You could choose to have it be used only by friend and family, only by other drivers who are rated five stars. You could choose to share it sometimes but not other times. That is one hundred percent what will occur. It's just a question of when,"[183] Elon said in his TED Talk, where he elaborated on some of his ideas about the future and the work involved in creating it.

> SpaceX president Gwynne Shotwell said that she thinks the first human will set foot on Mars by 2028. And when asked if Elon and Kimbal will travel to Mars together, Kimbal jumped at the chance to answer, "When we are ninety-five, what the hell else are we going to do?"[184]
>
> When it comes to solar, Elon thinks that in just fifteen years it will be unusual to see roofs without solar panels.

CHAPTER 15

GENIUS BOY

Maye Musk remembers that when her other two children would gaze at the moon, guessing it was millions of miles away, Elon was quick to step in with the precise distance. His little sister called him "Genius Boy."

That Genius Boy of long ago now has something in common with the comic book hero he read about in the adventures of Iron Man. Like Tony Stark, Elon has become known as a billionaire genius. And when disaster strikes or when lives are at stake or when people are facing serious problems that police and government can't solve, people ask Elon for help.

In Thailand, twelve boys ventured off to explore the country's longest cave with their soccer coach after practice, but torrential rain poured in behind them, flooding the cave and blocking their escape. They scrambled deeper into the cave to a dry ledge, but they were trapped, and no one knew exactly where.

Hours stretched to days, and the world watched exhausted cave divers, pained parents, and rescuers hold on to fleeting hope. And then people used Twitter to ask Elon directly for help. Couldn't he figure out a way to rescue these boys? That resulted in engineers from SpaceX, Tesla, and the Boring Company stopping their work and traveling to Asia to offer their expertise. They brought along a mini submarine made of rocket parts to carry the boys out of the cave. Ultimately, divers guided all twelve boys and their coach out without the minisub. But Elon left it in Thailand to use in future rescue missions.

Elon's minisub created a public relations crisis. One of the cavers who assisted with the rescue spoke with CNN and ridiculed the child-sized submarine, dismissing it as a publicity stunt and using crass innuendo to suggest what Elon could do with the submarine. The video clip went viral, and Elon responded angrily, calling the man a "pedo," short for pedophile. The caver has since filed a lawsuit, and as of this writing, the issue is far from settled.

As Elon was returning to the United States, another request came in, this one from Flint, Michigan. Could Elon help solve the years-long public water crisis that had poisoned thousands of children with lead? Elon promised to pay for water filters for every house affected and set up an e-mail to handle the requests. And in the same way Puerto Rico's governor reached out after Hurricane Maria, Flint's mayor reached out to Elon to discuss the city's specific needs. Elon and his foundation have since donated $480,000 to help Flint's schools get safe water.

MENDED FENCES? In October 2018, Justine Musk took to Twitter to thank Elon. A documentary was debuting about Congolese women, the violence they suffered, and their empowering path forward. Justine thanked Elon for his role and support in making sure the film was made. In return, Elon publicly thanked her for letting him know about it.

Just like Stark, Elon Musk is not your cookie-cutter superhero. He wasn't born with supernatural powers. He is flawed, gritty, intense. But he's also the person people turn to with their impossible dreams.

At yet another big press event, while Elon updated the crowd on the Big Falcon Rocket (aka Starship) and gushed about what the engineering team accomplished in building its engine, another billionaire stood offstage. His name was Yusaku Maezawa, but he likes to be called MZ.

Elon Musk, left, and Japanese billionaire Yusaku Maezawa at SpaceX headquarters in Hawthorne, California. (Photo by Chris Carlson/AP Photo.)

MZ approached Elon years ago with his greatest wish: to see the moon. Not just through a telescope. He'd already spent countless hours as a child, an adolescent, and a grown-up looking at the night sky, wondering about the moon, and letting the moonlight fire his imagination. He wanted to go to the moon in person. And he had an idea that going to the moon could lead to worldwide peace. This wasn't just a daydream, even though MZ didn't own a space company or have his own arsenal of moon-ready rockets. What he did have was the money to pay the enormous (and undisclosed) fare to make his lunar trip a reality.

And that led to this big moment at SpaceX: the announcement that MZ will become the first tourist to launch into space and fly around the moon. And not only that, he will take a group of artists with him. What might they create? They could inspire us, not as individuals from different countries, but as earthlings, united by the planet we share. These were MZ's questions. Choked up with emotion, he laid out his deepest desire, a desire shared and respected by the one man who could help him achieve it: Elon.

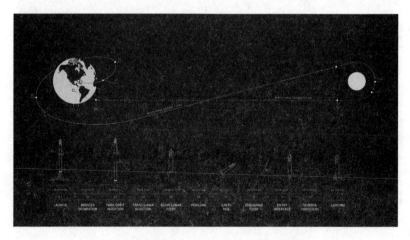

Proposed flight plan for the trip. (© SpaceX.)

Elon, too, was emotional when talking about this trip around the moon, because that dream is within reach.

"That someone is willing to do this," Elon said, squirming in his seat as he tried to control his feelings. "To take their money and help fund this new project that's risky, might not succeed, it's dangerous. He's like donating seats. These are great things. I tell you it's done a lot to restore my faith in humanity."[185]

There are still years of technological problems to solve before this mission launches. And Elon doesn't mince words about how dangerous it is; sending civilians into deep space aboard new technology could result in disaster. But fear is not going to paralyze Elon, whether solving this problem or the many others that he will take on.

Elon has described the daily deluge of thoughts as an ever-present explosion of ideas. It's impossible to predict what he'll tackle next. But his drive is unmistakable, as is his willingness to confront some of the biggest problems that exist on Earth and beyond.

Failure might be an option, but giving up is not.

ELON MUSK

NET WORTH: More than $23 billion

TITLES: Tesla (CEO), SpaceX (CEO), The Boring Company (CEO), Neurallink (CEO), Open AI (co-founder)

Got an interview with Elon? Better know the answer to this question. Rumor is he wants to know what was the biggest problem you faced, and how you solved it!

GARAGE: What's in Elon's garage? In addition to driving Teslas, Elon also owns a Jaguar Series 1 1967 E-Type Roadster and a Ford Model T given to him by a friend.

Elon Musk, June 14, 2018. (Photo by Kiichiro Sato, AP Photo.)

BIBLIOGRAPHY

Abramowitz, Rachel. "Robert Downey Jr. Is Ready to Play the Hero in 'Iron Man.'" *Los Angeles Times*, 27 April 2008. www.latimes.com/entertainment/la-ca-downey27apr27-story.html.

Anderson, Chris. "How Soon Is Now?" *Wired*, Nov. 2012. Reprinted in *The New Space Race: A Condé Nast Special Edition*, 2018, pp. 44–49.

Baer, Drake, and Shana Lebowitz. "14 Books That Inspired Elon Musk." *Business Insider*, 21 Oct. 2015. www.businessinsider.com/elon-musk-favorite-books-2015-10#the-hitchhikers-guide-to-the-galaxy-by-douglas-adams-2.

Belfiore, Michael P. *Rocketeers: How a Visionary Band of Business Leaders, Engineers, and Pilots Is Boldly Privatizing Space*. New York: Smithsonian Books, 2007.

Bloomberg Risk Takers. "Elon Musk: How I Became the Real 'Iron Man.'" 10 June 2014. YouTube video, 44:59. youtu.be/mh45igK4Esw.

Boring Company. "The Chicago Express Loop." www.boringcompany.com/chicago/.

Boudette, Neal E., and Raymond Zhong. "Tesla Model Y, a New S.U.V., Is Unveiled Amid Mounting Challenges." *The New York Times*, 15 March 2019, www.nytimes.com/2019/03/15/business/tesla-model-y.html.

Brooks, Mel, dir. *Spaceballs*. Beverly Hills, CA: Metro-Goldwyn-Mayer. 1987.

Burning Man Project. "First-Timer's Guide." burningman.org/event/preparation/first-timers-guide/.

Campbell, Andy. "SpaceX's Successful Landing Means You and I Might Go to Space Sometime Soon." *HuffPost*, 22 Dec. 2015. www.huffingtonpost.com/entry/spacexs-successful-landing-means-you-and-might-go-to-space_us_567968aee4b06fa6887ea04a.

CBS News. "Tesla CEO Elon Musk, Stressed but 'Optimistic,' Predicts Big Increase in Model 3 Production." *CBS This Morning*, 13 April 2018. www.cbsnews.com/news/elon-musk-tesla-model-3-problems-interview-today-2018-04-13/.

Cellan-Jones, Rory. "Stephen Hawking Warns Artificial Intelligence Could End Mankind." BBC News, 2 Dec. 2014. www.bbc.com/news/technology-30290540.

Chang, Kenneth. "First Private Craft Docks with Space Station." *New York Times*, 25 May 2012. nyti.ms/2p06S4L.

Cofield, Calla. "Elon Musk Shows Childlike Joy (and Dread) in Rocket-Landing Video." Space.com, 22 Dec. 2016. shar.es/a1N6uQ.

Crowley Redding, Anna. *Google It: A History of Google*. New York: Feiwel and Friends, 2018.

D'Angelo, Chris. "SpaceX Makes History with 'Insane' Launch, Proving Rockets Can Be Reused." *Huffington Post*, 22 Dec. 2015. www.huffingtonpost.com/entry/spacex-history-rockets-reused_us_5678aefee4b014efe0d69a72.

Davies, Alex. "MAPS: Here's Tesla's Plan to Cover America in Superchargers." *Business Insider*, 30 May 2013. www.businessinsider.com/maps-of-teslas-supercharger-network-2013-5.

Davis, Johnny. "One More Giant Leap." *Telegraph* (London), 4 Aug. 2007. www.telegraph.co.uk/culture/3666994/One-more-giant-leap.html.

Dornoch Cathedral. "Welcome." www.dornoch-cathedral.com/index.html.

Elliott, Hannah. "Elon Musk to Divorce from Wife Talulah Riley." *Forbes*, 18 Jan. 2012. www.forbes.com/sites/hannahelliott/2012/01/18/elon-musk-to-divorce-wife-talulah-riley/#6b5d8e9571b2.

Emanuel, Rahm. "Boring Company Chicago O'Hare Announcement." News conference with Elon Musk in Chicago, 14 June 2018. YouTube video, 28:09. youtu.be/CnobWh5iloE.

Erwin, Sandra. "SpaceX Wins $130 Million Military Launch Contract for Falcon Heavy Rocket." Space.com, 24 June 2018. shar.es/a1NCjP.

Etherington, Darrell. "Tesla Officially Acquires SolarCity." TechCrunch, 21 Nov. 2016. tcrn.ch/2gaNhKW.

Fernholz, Tim. *Rocket Billionaires: Elon Musk, Jeff Bezos, and the New Space Race*. New York: Houghton Mifflin Harcourt, 2018.

Friend, Tad. "Plugged In: Can Elon Musk Lead the Way to an Electric-Car Future?" *New Yorker*, 24 Aug. 2009. www.newyorker.com/magazine/2009/08/24/plugged-in.

Gaiman, Neil. "What Was He Like, Douglas Adams?" Foreword to *The Ultimate Hitchhiker's Guide to the Galaxy: Five Novels in One Outrageous Volume*, by Douglas Adams. New York: Ballantine Books, 2002.

Garcia, Mark, ed. "Space Debris and Human Spacecraft." NASA, 7 Aug. 2017. www.nasa.gov/mission_pages/station/news/orbital_debris.html.

Giving Pledge. givingpledge.org.

Hahm, Melody. "Elon Musk is Losing the Confidence of Employees, Survey Says." *Yahoo! Finance*, Yahoo!, 5 Mar. 2019. finance.yahoo.com/news/Teslas-spacex-blind-survey-211329818.html.

Harris, Mark. "First Space, Then Auto—Now Elon Musk Quietly Tinkers with Education." Ars Technica, 25 June 2018. arstechnica.com/science/2018/06/first-space-then-auto-now-elon-musk-quietly-tinkers-with-education/.

Harwood, William. "SpaceX Pulls off Dramatic Falcon 9 Launch, Landing." CBS News, 21 Dec. 2015. www.cbsnews.com/news/spacex-pulls-off-dramatic-falcon-9-launch-landing/.

Hotz, Robert Lee. "Mars Probe Lost Due to Simple Math Error." *Los Angeles Times*, 1 Oct. 1999. articles.latimes.com/1999/oct/01/news/mn-17288.

Huynh, Tuan, and Andrew London. "Tesla Model 3 Release Date, News and Features." TechRadar, 2 Nov. 2017. www.techradar.com/news/tesla-model-3.

Junod, Tom. "Elon Musk: Triumph of His Will." *Esquire*, 14 Nov. 2012. www.esquire.com/news-politics/a16681/elon-musk-interview-1212/.

Kanellos, Michael. "Electric Sports Car Packs a Punch, but Will It Sell?" Road Show, 21 July 2006. www.cnet.com/roadshow/news/electric-sports-car-packs-a-punch-but-will-it-sell/.

Keith, Lori. "Though Shuttle Retired, International Space Station Still Open for Business, Research Going Strong." NASA, 27 Feb. 2012. www.nasa.gov/mission_pages/station/research/news/iss_vehicles.html.

Lambert, Fred. "Tesla Dedicates New Speed Limiting Feature to 18-Yr-Old Who Died in a Model S Crash." Electrek, 26 June 2018, electrek.co/2018/06/26/tesla-dedicates-new-speed-limiting-feature-kid-died-model-s-crash/.

———. "Tesla Has 'About 11,000' Energy Storage Projects Underway in Puerto Rico, Says Elon Musk." Electrek, 3 June 2018. electrek.co/2018/06/03/tesla-energy-storage-projects-puerto-rico-elon-musk/.

———. "Understanding Tesla's New Supercharger Access for Model S and Model X." Electrek, 20 May 2017. electrek.co/2017/05/20/tesla-new-supercharger-model-s-model-x/.

Lewin, Lyric, Brett Roegiers, Bernadette Tuazon, and Kyle Almond. "In Pictures: Hurricane Maria Pummels Puerto Rico." CNN, 2017. www.cnn.com/interactive/2017/09/world/hurricane-maria-puerto-rico-cnnphotos/.

Loder, Natasha. "Mother of Invention." *1843*, Feb./March 2018. www.1843magazine.com/features/mother-of-invention.

Malik, Tariq. "Elon Musk Was Emotionally Wrecked by SpaceX's 1st Crew Dragon Launch Success— But In A Good Way." *Space.com*, 2 March 2019. www.space.com/elon-musk-spacex-crew-dragon-test-launch-success.html.

Martin, Chris. "Solar Has Overtaken Gas and Wind as Biggest Source of New U.S. Power." Bloomberg, 12 June 2018. www.bloomberg.com/news/articles/2018-06-12/solar-surpasses-gas-and-wind-as-biggest-source-of-new-u-s-power.

Matousek, Mark. "Elon Musk Reveals New Details About Tesla's Plans to Build Gigafactories Around the World." *Business Insider*, 6 June 2018. www.businessinsider.com/elon-musk-details-teslas-gigafactory-plans-in-us-china-europe-2018-6.

McGivern, Mark. "St Trinians Star Talulah Riley Marries Internet Millionaire in Fairytale Highland Wedding." *Daily Record* (Glasgow, Scotland), 28 Sept. 2010. www.dailyrecord.co.uk/entertainment/celebrity/st-trinians-star-talulah-riley-1071170.

"Model Y." *Tesla, Inc*, 15 March 2019, www.tesla.com/presskit.

Molina, Brett. "Tesla Delivers Solar Power to Puerto Rico Hospital." *USA Today*, 27 Oct. 2017. usat.ly/2zHy36b.

Morris, Charles. "The Definitive Story of Tesla's Beginnings, Told by Co-Founder Marc Tarpenning." *Tesla News* (blog). EVANNEX, 18 June 2017. evannex.com/blogs/news/the-definitive-story-of-tesla-s-beginnings-told-by-co-founder-marc-tarpenning.

Musgrove, Mike. "An Electric Car with Juice." *Washington Post*, 22 July 2006. www.washingtonpost.com/wp-dyn/content/article/2006/07/21/AR2006072101515.html.

Musk, Elon. "Am considering taking Tesla private at $420. Funding secured." Twitter, 7 Aug. 2018. twitter.com/elonmusk/status/1026872652290379776.

———. "The Boring Company Information Session." Los Angeles, 17 May 2018. YouTube video, 57:55. youtu.be/AwX9G38vdCE.

———. Interview by Alison van Diggelen. "An Evening with Elon Musk." Computer History Museum, Mountain View, CA, 23 Jan. 2013. YouTube video, 1:16:51. youtu.be/AHHwXUm3iIg.

———. Interview by Chris Anderson. "The Future We're Building—and Boring." TED2017 conference, April 2017. TED Talk video, 40:51. www.ted.com/talks/elon_musk_the_future_we_re_building_and_boring.

———. Interview by Joe Rogan. *Joe Rogan Experience* (podcast). Episode 1169, 7 Sept. 2018. YouTube video, 2:37:02. youtu.be/ycPr5-27vSI.

———. Interview by Kevin Rose. "Foundation 20 // Elon Musk." 7 Sept. 2012. YouTube video, 26:42. youtu.be/L-s_3b5fRd8.

———. Interview by Mohammad Abdullah Al Gergawi. World Government Summit. Dubai, United Arab Emirates, 13 Feb. 2017. YouTube video, 35:49. youtu.be/lbkO2a2T6Cs.

———. Interview by Neil deGrasse Tyson. "The Future of Humanity with Elon Musk." *StarTalk Radio*. 22 March 2015. Audio, 50:25. www.startalkradio.net/show/the-future-of-humanity-with-elon-musk/.

———. Interview by Sal Khan. "Elon Musk—CEO of Tesla Motors and SpaceX." Khan Academy, 17 April 2013. Video, 48:41. www.khanacademy.org/talks-and-interviews/khan-academy-living-room-chats/v/elon-musk.

———. Interview by Sarah Lacy. "PandoMonthly: Fireside Chat with Elon Musk." 17 July 2012. YouTube video, 1:03:10, youtu.be/uegOUmgKB4E.

———. "More background: I arrived in North America at 17 w $2000, a backpack & a suitcase full of books. Paid my own way thru college." Twitter, 9 June 2018, 6:33 p.m. twitter.com/elonmusk/status/1005593651219582977.

———. "Supercharger Announcement." Tesla Motors Inc., 30 May 2013. Video, 1:50. player.vimeo.com/video/66853584.

———. "What's actually amazing about this accident is that a Model S hit a fire truck at 60mph and the driver only broke an ankle." Twitter, 14 May 2018, 3:57 p.m. twitter.com/elonmusk/status/996132429772410882.

———. "Yeah, worked on my cousin's farm for six weeks around my 18th birthday. I was so kewl." Twitter, 25 Jan. 2019. twitter.com/elonmusk/status/1088864971885207552

Musk, Elon, and Kimbal Musk. Interview by Jeff Skoll. Milken Institute Global Conference, 29 April 2013. YouTube video, 45:55. youtu.be/1u6kQIzzaPI.

Musk, Justine. "'I Was a Starter Wife': Inside America's Messiest Divorce." *Marie Claire*, 29 March 2018. www.marieclaire.com/sex-love/a5380/millionaire-starter-wife/.

———. "Very pleased + proud that my ex -- you might have heard of him -- helped get this documentary made about (one of my heroines) Eve Ensler." Twitter, 9 Oct. 2018. twitter.com/justinemusk/status/1049512433834844161.

Musk, Kimbal. Interview by Susan Adams. "Kimbal Musk on How Silicon Valley Taught Him to Run Restaurants and Why His Brother Elon Will Win," Trep Talks, *Forbes*, 14 July 2016. www.forbes.com/sites/forbestreptalks/2016/07/14/kimbal-musk-on-how-silicon-valley-taught-him-to-run-restaurants-and-why-his-brother-elon-will-win/.

National Geographic. "Exclusive: Watch Elon Musk Freak Out over the Falcon Heavy Launch." Cape Canaveral, FL, 6 Feb. 2018. Video, 1:37. news.nationalgeographic.com/2018/02/elon-musk-reacts-spacex-falcon-heavy-launch-space-science/.

———. "SpaceX Makes History | MARS." Cape Canaveral, FL. Posted 19 Dec. 2016. YouTube video, 3:55. youtu.be/brE21SBO2j8.

National Transportation Safety Board. *Preliminary Report Highway HWY18FH011* (accident 23 March 2018, Mountain View, CA), 7 June 2018. www.ntsb.gov/investigations/AccidentReports/Reports/HWY18FH011-preliminary.pdf.

———. *Preliminary Report Highway HWY18FH013* (accident 8 May 2018, Fort Lauderdale, FL), 26 June 2018. www.ntsb.gov/investigations/AccidentReports/Reports/HWY18FH013-prelim.pdf.

Neuralink Corp. www.neuralink.com.

O'Callaghan, Jonathan. "The Elon Musk Project You've Never Heard of That Might Change the World." IFLScience, 21 June 2017. www.iflscience.com/technology/the-elon-musk-project-youve-never-heard-of-that-might-change-the-world/.

———. "Elon Musk Unveils the Ridiculously Big Tesla Gigfactory." IFLScience, 28 April 2016. www.iflscience.com/technology/elon-musk-unveils-the-ridiculously-big-tesla-gigfactory/.

Olsen, Patrick. "Tesla Model 3 Gets CR Recommendation After Braking Update." *Consumer Reports*, 30 May 2018. www.consumerreports.org/car-safety/tesla-model-3-gets-cr-recommendation-after-braking-update/.

OpenAI. openai.com.

Oremus, Will. "Elon Musk Is Not a Comic Book Superhero. He's Way More Interesting Than That." Slate, 21 May 2015. slate.com/articles/business/moneybox/2015/05/elon_musk_biography_review_how_did_a_sci_fi_nut_with_a_hero_complex_becoming.html.

———. "Romney Decides That Thriving Electric-Car Start-up Tesla Is a 'Loser.'" Slate, 4 Oct. 2012, slate.com/technology/2012/10/mitt-romney-calls-tesla-loser-like-solyndra-in-presidential-debate.html.

Paine, Chris, dir. *Do You Trust This Computer?* Papercut Films, 5 April 2018. doyoutrustthiscomputer.org/watch.

Paris Productions. "EV1 Funeral," part 1, Hollywood, CA, July 24, 2003. Posted by EV1Forever. YouTube video, 8:00. youtu.be/HZHka8KUj74.

Pelley, Scott. "SpaceX: Entrepreneur's Race to Space." Produced by Harry Radcliffe. Script of *60 Minutes* segment, 18 March 2012. www.cbsnews.com/news/spacex-entrepreneurs-race-to-space.

———. "Tesla and SpaceX: Elon Musk's Industrial Empire." Produced by Harry Radcliffe. Script of *60 Minutes* segment, 30 March 2014. www.cbsnews.com/news/tesla-and-spacex-elon-musks-industrial-empire/.

Peters, Adele. "During Puerto Rico's Blackout, Solar Microgrids Kept the Lights On." Fast Company, 25 April 2018. www.fastcompany.com/40562660/during-puerto-ricos-blackout-solar-microgrids-kept-the-lights-on.

Queen's University. "Quick Facts." www.queensu.ca/about/quickfacts.

Ralph, Eric. "Elon Musk Reveals SpaceX's New Scifi-Inspired Drone Ship—A Shortfall of Gravitas." Teslarati, 12 Feb. 2018. www.teslarati.com/spacex-new-drone-ship-a-shortfall-of-gravitas/.

Ressi, Adeo. "About." www.adeoressi.com/index.php/about/.

Rive, Lyndon. Interview by Brian Dumaine. "SolarCity's Burning Man Roots." *Fortune*, 9 Oct. 2014. Video, 1:15. fortune.com/video/2014/10/09/solarcitys-burning-man-roots/.

———. "Turning Toward the Sun." *New York Times*, 20 April 2013. nyti.ms/11peOqU.

Robertson, Adi. "Tesla Repays $465 Million Government Green Energy Loan Ahead of Schedule." Verge, 22 May 2013. www.theverge.com/2013/5/22/4356860/tesla-repays-465-million-government-green-energy-loan.

Schwartz, John. "Launch of Private Rocket Fails; Three Satellites Were Onboard." *New York Times*, 3 Aug. 2008. nyti.ms/2yRQIyd.

Severson, Kim. "Kimbal Musk Wants to Feed America, Silicon Valley–Style." *New York Times*, 16 Oct. 2017. nyti.ms/2kQUWBI.

Shotwell, Gwynne. Interview by Chris Anderson. "SpaceX's Plan to Fly You Across the Globe in 30 Minutes." TED2018 conference, April 2018. TED Talk video, 21:31. www.ted.com/talks/gwynne_shotwell_spacex_s_plan_to_fly_you_across_the_globe_in_30_minutes.

Singel, Ryan. "Ouch: Romney Calls Tesla a 'Loser.'" *Wired*, 3 Oct. 2012. www.wired.com/2012/10/romney-tesla-loser/.

Smithsonian National Museum of American History. "EV1 Electric Car, 1997." *America on the Move* exhibition. americanhistory.si.edu/collections/search/object/nmah_1293145.

SpaceX. www.spacex.com.

———. "The Falcon Has Landed." Falcon 9 launch and landing, 21 Dec. 2015. Posted 12 Jan. 2016. YouTube video, 3:37. youtu.be/ANv5UfZsvZQ.

———. "First Private Passenger on Lunar BFR Mission." News conference, 28 Sept. 2018. YouTube video, 1:44:12. youtu.be/zu7WJD8vpAQ.

Stangel, Luke. "Both SolarCity Founders Have Now Quit Tesla, Just Months After $2.6B Acquisition Closed." *Silicon Valley Business Journal*, 19 July 2017. www.bizjournals.com/sanjose/news/2017/07/19/tesla-tsla-solarcity-peter-lyndon-rive-acquisition.html.

Strauss, Neil. "Elon Musk: The Architect of Tomorrow." *Rolling Stone*, 15 Nov. 2017. www. rollingstone.com/culture/features/elon-musk-inventors-plans-for-outer-space-cars-finding-love-w511747.

Tarpenning, Marc. "Tesla's High Speed Innovation." Lecture at Product Leader Summit, Redwood City, CA, 19 May 2017. youtu.be/UOt9KF2fsdw.

Tesla Inc. www.tesla.com.

———. "Tesla Semi & Roadster Unveil." Product announcement, 16 Nov. 2017. YouTube video, 35:03. youtu.be/5RRmepp7i5g.

Tesla Motors Inc. "Tesla Model X Reveal." Product announcement, 9 Feb. 2012. YouTube video, 25:27. youtu.be/mURbzh9t0_0.

Urban, Tim. "The Elon Musk Post Series." Wait but Why, 28 March 2017. waitbutwhy.com/2017/03/elon-musk-post-series.html.

Vance, Ashlee. *Elon Musk: Tesla, SpaceX, and the Quest for a Fantastic Future*. New York: Ecco, 2015.

Vital, Anna. "How Elon Musk Started." Infographic. *Adioma* (blog), 23 Feb. 2016. blog.adioma.com/how-elon-musk-started-infographic/.

von Holzhausen, Franz. "More Than Electric." Keynote presentation. Autodesk University Conference, 8 Dec. 2010. YouTube video, 8:52. youtu.be/AyQ4SOCHAYA.

Wall, Mike. "Wow! SpaceX Lands Orbital Rocket Successfully in Historic First." Space.com, 21 Dec. 2015. shar.es/a1LvfE.

Wang, Christine. "Tesla Voluntarily Recalls 123,000 Model S Cars over Faulty Steering Component." CNBC, 29 March 2018. www.cnbc.com/2018/03/29/tesla-recalls-123000-model-s-cars-over-potential-power-steering-failure-reports.html.

Wattles, Jackie. "NTSB: Tesla Driver Did Not Have Hands on Wheel Before Fatal Crash." CNN Business, 7 June 2018. shar.es/a1LvdW.

Wong, Julia Carrie. "Tesla factory Workers Reveal Pain, Injury and Stress: 'Everything Feels like the Future but Us.'" *Guardian* (Manchester, England), 18 May 2017. www.theguardian.com/technology/2017/may/18/tesla-workers-factory-conditions-elon-musk.

Zhao, Helen. "California Workplace Safety Agency Opens Probe into Tesla." CNBC, 18 April 2018. www.cnbc.com/2018/04/18/california-workplace-safety-agency-opens-probe-into-tesla.html.

Zipkin, Nina. "Tosca Musk, the Youngest Sibling of the Famous Family, Talks Romance, Problem-Solving and Growing Up Musk." *Entrepreneur*. 14 Feb. 2018. entm.ag/03j.

ENDNOTES

1. Vance, *Elon Musk*, p. 31.

2. Vance, p. 32.

3. Elon Musk, interview by Alison van Diggelen.

4. Elon Musk, interview by van Diggelen.

5. Strauss, "Elon Musk."

6. Friend, "Plugged In."

7. Strauss, "Elon Musk."

8. Vance, p. 24.

9. Vance, p. 33.

10. Strauss, "Elon Musk."

11. Strauss, "Elon Musk."

12. Elon Musk, interview by Neil deGrasse Tyson.

13. Vance, p. 38.

14. Vance, p. 38.

15. Vance, p. 38.

16. Elon Musk, interview by Neil deGrasse Tyson.

17. Vance, p. 37

18. Strauss, "Elon Musk."

19. Vance, p. 37.

20. Vance, p. 37.

21. Strauss, "Elon Musk."

22. Elon Musk, interview by Alison van Diggelen.

23. Strauss, "Elon Musk."

24. Junod, "Elon Musk."

25. Junod, "Elon Musk."

26. Elon Musk and Kimbal Musk, interview by Jeff Skoll.

27. Friend, "Plugged In."

28. Elon Musk, interview by Alison van Diggelen.

29. Belfiore, *Rocketeers*, p. 171.

30. Elon Musk, interview by Alison van Diggelen.

31. Elon Musk, interview by Neil deGrasse Tyson.

32. Elon Musk, interview by Tyson.

33. Vance, *Elon Musk*, p. 46.

34. Vance, p. 50.

35. Vance, p. 48.

36. Vance, p. 47

37. Vance, p. 77.

38. Vance, p. 53.

39. Elon Musk, interview by Sal Khan.

40. Elon Musk, interview by Khan.

41. Elon Musk, interview by Khan.

42. Elon Musk, interview by Khan.

43. Elon Musk and Kimbal Musk, interview by Jeff Skoll.

44. Musk and Musk, interview.

45. Elon Musk, interview by Sal Khan.

46. Junod, "Elon Musk."

47. Musk and Musk, interview by Jeff Skoll.

48. Musk and Musk, interview.

49. van Diggelen, Alison. "Transcript of Elon Musk Interview: Iron Man, Growing up in South Africa." Fresh Dialogues, 7 Feb.

50. Elon Musk, interview by Alison van Diggelen.

51. Musk and Musk, interview by Jeff Skoll.

52. Musk and Musk, interview by Jeff Skoll.

53. Musk and Musk, interview by Jeff Skoll.

54. Musk and Musk, interview by Jeff Skoll.

55. Musk and Musk, interview by Jeff Skoll.

56. Musk and Musk, interview by Jeff Skoll.

57. Elon Musk, interview by Sal Khan.

58. Elon Musk, interview by Alison van Diggelen.

59. Junod, "Elon Musk."

60. Elon Musk, interview by Alison van Diggelen.

61. Vance, p. 96

62. Vance, p. 95.

63. Kimbal Musk, interview by Susan Adams.

64. Musk and Musk, interview by Jeff Skoll.

65. Elon Musk, interview by Sal Khan.

66. Strauss, "Elon Musk."

67. Elon Musk, interview by Sal Khan.

68. Elon Musk, interview by Sal Khan.

69. Elon Musk, interview by Sal Khan.

70. Elon Musk, interview by Sarah Lacy.

71. Elon Musk, interview by Alison van Diggelen.

72. Junod, "Elon Musk."

73. Elon Musk, interview by Sarah Lacy.

74. Elon Musk, interview by Sal Khan.

75. Elon Musk, interview by Sal Khan.

76. Junod, "Elon Musk."

77. Elon Musk, interview by Sal Khan.

78. SpaceX.com/about

79. Elon Musk, interview by Sarah Lacy.

80. Shotwell, interview by Chris Anderson. "SpaceX's Plan to Fly."

81. Junod, "Elon Musk."

82. Paris Productions, "EV1 Funeral."

83. Elon Musk, interview by Alison van Diggelen.

84. Elon Musk, interview by Alison van Diggelen.

85. Elon Musk, interview by Alison van Diggelen.

86. Elon Musk, interview by Alison van Diggelen.

87. Elon Musk, interview by Sarah Lacy.

88. Elon Musk, interview by Kevin Rose.

89. Elon Musk, interview by Sarah Lacy.

90. Tarpenning, "Tesla's High Speed Innovation."

91. Vance, p. 148.

92. Rive, "Turning Toward the Sun."

93. Elon Musk, interview by Alison van Diggelen.

94. Elon Musk, interview by Alison van Diggelen.

95. Elon Musk, interview by Joe Rogan.

96. Urban, "The Elon Musk Post Series."

97. Gaiman, "What Was He Like?"

98. Vance, p. 140.

99. Justine Musk, "I Was a Starter Wife."

100. Vance, p. 186.

101. Kanellos, "Electric Sports Car Packs a Punch."

102. Musgrove, "An Electric Car with Juice."

103. Shotwell, "SpaceX's Plan."

104. Shotwell, "SpaceX's Plan."

105. Vance, p. 173.

106. Elon Musk, interview by Sarah Lacy.

107. Vance, p. 193.

108. Musk and Musk, interview by Jeff Skoll.

109. Junod, "Elon Musk."

110. Vance, p. 203.

111. Vance, p. 203.

112. Elon Musk, interview by Kevin Rose.

113. Elon Musk, interview by Sarah Lacy.

114. Vance, p. 206.

115. Junod, "Triumph of His Will."

116. Vance, p. 210.

117. Tesla Inc., www.tesla.com/autopilot.

118. Elon Musk, interview by Kevin Rose.

119. Elon Musk, interview by Sarah Lacy.

120. Elon Musk, interview by Sarah Lacy.

121. Elon Musk, interview by Sarah Lacy.

122. Elon Musk, interview by Alison van Diggelen.

123. Elon Musk, "@rileytalulah."

124. Elliott, "Elon Musk to Divorce."

125. Tesla Motors Inc., "Tesla Model X Reveal."

126. Oremus, "Romney Decides."

127. Robertson, "Tesla Repays $465 Million."

128. Bloomberg, "Elon Musk."

129. Elon Musk, interview by Chris Anderson.

130. Elon Musk, interview by Alison van Diggelen.

131. D'Angelo, "SpaceX Makes History."

132. Campbell, "SpaceX's Successful Landing."

133. Strauss, "Elon Musk."

134. Strauss, "Elon Musk."

135. Strauss, "Elon Musk."

136. Tarpenning, "Tesla's High Speed Innovation."

137. National Geographic, "Exclusive: Watch Elon Musk."

138. Chang, "First Private Craft."

139. Elon Musk, interview by Alison van Diggelen.

140. Shotwell, "SpaceX's Plan to Fly."

141. Shotwell, interview by Chris Anderson.

142. Shotwell, interview by Chris Anderson.

143. Shotwell, interview by Chris Anderson.

144. Shotwell, interview by Chris Anderson.

145. Vance, p. 365.

146. Elon Musk, interview by Chris Anderson.

147. Elon Musk, interview by Chris Anderson.

148. Elon Musk, "The Boring Company Information Session."

149. Elon Musk, "The Boring Company Information Session."

150. Elon Musk, "The Boring Company Information Session."

151. Elon Musk, interview by Chris Anderson.

152. Elon Musk, "The Boring Company Information Session."

153. Elon Musk, "The Boring Company Information Session."

154. Elon Musk, interview by Joe Rogan.

155. Brooks, *Spaceballs*.

156. Elon Musk, interview by Joe Rogan.

157. Emanuel, "Boring Company Chicago O'Hare."

158. Emanuel, "Boring Company Chicago O'Hare."

159. Elon Musk, interview by Sal Khan.

160. Elon Musk, interview by Sal Khan.

161. Elon Musk, "The Boring Company Information Session."

162. Elon Musk, interview by Chris Anderson.

163. Elon Musk, "The Boring Company Information Session."

164. Vance, p. 43.

165. Strauss, "Elon Musk."

166. Paine, *Do You Trust This Computer?*

167. Paine, *Do You Trust This Computer?*

168. Cellan-Jones, "Stephen Hawking Warns."

169. Elon Musk, interview by Joe Rogan.

170. OpenAI, openai.com.

171. Elon Musk, interview by Joe Rogan.

172. Paine, *Do You Trust This Computer?*

173. Elon Musk, interview by Joe Rogan.

174. Neuralink, www.neuralink.com.

175. Elon Musk, interview by Mohammad Abdullah Al Gergawi.

176. Elon Musk, interview by Mohammad Abdullah Al Gergawi.

177. Elon Musk, interview by Chris Anderson.

178. CBS News, "Tesla CEO Elon Musk."

179. Wong, "Tesla Factory Workers Reveal Pain."

180. Elon Musk, "What's actually amazing."

181. Elon Musk, "Am considering taking Tesla."

182. Elon Musk, interview by Chris Anderson.

183. Elon Musk, interview by Chris Anderson.

184. Musk and Musk, interview by Jeff Skoll.

185. SpaceX, "First Private Passenger."

ACKNOWLEDGMENTS

When I first dug into the details of Elon's life, one story stood out in particular—the time school bullies kicked Elon down a flight of stairs and beat him unconscious. It was a stunning blow for a young boy. And yet, he found the strength to keep going, continue being himself, and connect to a bigger vision for his life. The fact is that we will all face challenges and life events that feel insurmountable and painful. But my wish for you, Dear Reader, is that when you are discouraged, disillusioned, or mistreated—that you never give up. Get up. Tend your wounds. And keep going. The world needs you. Perhaps, like Elon, you'll also find your refuge in books, in stories that set your gaze on the horizon and all the possibility that exists for your life. There are so many of us cheering you on, excited about what you have to offer this planet (and beyond!).

I have so many people who have rallied around me, and I owe a debt of gratitude to my friends, family, and colleagues. Let me start with my editor, the brilliant Holly West. Thank you, Holly, for trusting me with such an incredible idea and leading the way as we shaped and honed a book that I hope will leave our readers feeling empowered and excited. Thank you. To the entire team at Feiwel & Friends, thank you for your hard work, attention to detail, and enthusiasm for this book. Also, to the team at SpaceX, thank you for your help with this project.

My agent, Ammi-Joan Paquette, is not only talented and one of the hardest-working people I know, but she is also a terrific person and a dear friend. I am grateful beyond words to Joan and the entire Erin Murphy Literary Agency team and Gangos!

My critique partners have been with me through every high and low, every rejection, and every book deal (yay!). To Melanie Ellsworth, Laurie Warchol, Helen Stevens, Darlene Ivy, and Vivian Kirkfield—thank you.

To librarians and teachers everywhere, you quite simply make the world go around. Thank you for your support in getting books about STEM, innovation, and the human stories behind these companies into readers' hands. Your support is important. And your example of tireless devotion to your students humbles me.

My girlfriends, near and far, are the kind who bring you flowers just because, make you belly laugh, text you nerdy articles, ask you how your writing is going (and then listen through the long, painful answer). They are the kind who pick up your kids, rake snow off your roof, and cheer you on because they really believe in you. I love you all, each and every one. And, Pete, that includes you, too.

To my friend, David Sammarco, thank you for supporting my efforts and lending your expertise to the book. To my brother, Patrick Crowley, it's been such fun sharing this journey with you. Thank you for your careful and insightful read of this manuscript. And thanks to my sister-in-law, Dr. Lisa Rosenfelt, who is a devoted champion of girls and women in STEM, including those who write about it—lucky me! To Tim and Kelsey Crowley, thank you for your love and support. To my father, James Crowley, thank you for every word of comfort and encouragement—all three trillion of them! To Marianne and David, thank you for never doubting me, ever. To my stepsister, Erica, you are the gift of a lifetime, and I am so grateful for you. To my friend and co-parent, Mike, thank you.

And to two of the most interesting and spectacular creatures on the planet, Crowley and Quinn, a mother could not ask for more. Thank you for your tremendous support. It's just delightful to watch you follow your own interests and passions. Can't wait to see where they lead you.

Last but not least, to everyone pushing the limits of technology, science, math, engineering, and physics to solve some of the biggest problems that exist and answer some of the biggest questions humanity faces (and in the process, change the world for the better), thank you. Your work is inspiring the next generation. What a legacy.

Don't miss these other inspiring titles from
Anna Crowley Redding:

From a college project made out of knock-off Legos to one of the most influential companies in the world, award-winning investigative reporter Anna Redding shares the true story of Google, its history, its innovations, and where it will take us next.

In April 2019, the Event Horizon Telescope Team unveiled the first *ever* image of a supermassive black hole. Based off extensive research and hours of interviews with many of the team's groundbreaking scientists, physicists, and mathematicians, *Black Hole Chasers* is a story of unique technological innovation and scientific breakthroughs, but more importantly, it's a story of human curiosity and triumph.

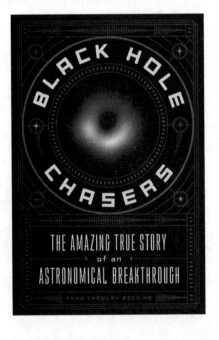